WHERE PEOPLE FEAST

To Bob & Darlene,
Have fun with
the recipes!

Annie!

Dolly Watts McRae

WHERE PEOPLE FEAST

An Indigenous People's Cookbook

by Dolly and Annie Watts

ARSENAL
PULP PRESS

WHERE PEOPLE FEAST

ARSENAL PULP PRESS
Suite 200, 341 Water Street
Vancouver, BC
Canada V6B 1B8
arsenalpulp.com

The publisher gratefully acknowledges the support of the Government of Canada through the Book Publishing Industry Development Program and the Government of British Columbia through the Book Publishing Tax Credit Program for its publishing activities.

The authors and publisher assert that the information contained in this book is true and complete to the best of their knowledge. All recommendations are made without guarantee on the part of the authors and publisher. The authors and publisher disclaim any liability in connection with the use of this information. For more information, contact the publisher.

Text and cover design by Lisa Eng-Lodge, Electra Design Group
Production assistance by Andrea Schmidt
Photography by Pamela Bethel, with the exception of the image on page 151, by Svetlana Chistyakova
Illustrations by Annie Watts, with the exception of the owl emblem by Tamara Bell and spoon
    emblem by Lyle Wilson

Printed and bound in Canada

Library and Archives Canada Cataloguing in Publication:
Watts, Dolly, 1935-
    Where people feast : an indigenous people's cookbook / Dolly and
Annie Watts.
Includes index.
ISBN-13: 978-1-55152-221-0
ISBN-10: 1-55152-221-7
    1. Indian cookery. I. Watts, Annie. II. Title.
TX715.6.W375 2007   641.59'297   C2006-907012-1

Contents

I would like to dedicate this book to my late mother Martha Morgan and my mother-in-law Louise Watts who taught me a lot about cooking.

— Dolly Watts, Chief Lian

Acknowledgements

We would like to express our deepest gratitude
to the brilliant team at Arsenal Pulp Press who worked
diligently to help make this book a reality. Next, we
would like to thank our families, friends, and guests who
have supported our efforts all these years. Finally, we
would like to thank all the people who hosted our cooking classes and wrote about this cookbook.

MAP OF BRITISH COLUMBIA

This map includes the First Nations Territories and other points of interest mentioned in the book.

SCALE: 1 CM = 61 KM | 1 INCH = 93 MILES

ALASKA

YUKON

NORTHWEST TERRITORIES

Gitk'san

Nisga'a

Nass River

Skeena River

KITWANGA

PRINCE RUPERT

Tsimshian

BRITISH COLUMBIA

ALBERTA

Shuswap

Kwakiutl

Lillooet

Thompson River

Nuu-chah-nulth

PORT ALBERNI

Okanagan

Coast Salish

VANCOUVER

CANADA
UNITED STATES

Makah

VICTORIA

SEATTLE

N

PACIFIC OCEAN

WASHINGTON

Introduction

Welcome to **WHERE PEOPLE FEAST**, a cookbook that sheds light on the unique culinary traditions and cooking techniques of Native American people who live along the Pacific Northwest Coast of British Columbia, Canada. This collection shows how to prepare and preserve wild game, seafood, vegetables, fruits, and unusual ingredients such as oolichan, herring roe, and sopalali berries, (all of which can be purchased on-line from distributors if not from your local specialty or gourmet markets). The foods and culinary traditions from two areas in particular are featured, which make up the main cultural heritage of the authors, Dolly and Annie Watts. The first is the Gitk'san Nation territory (approximately 27,000 acres/110 square kilometers) in central British Columbia, which has two great rivers, the Bulkley and the Skeena, that pass through it. Located 750 miles (1,200 kilometers) away from Vancouver, the Gitk'san territory is truly a place of plenty, so much so that the Gitk'san people consider that they live in Tda'im'lax'amid, or "situated on a nice place." The second area featured in the book is the Nuu-chah-nulth (formerly "Nootka") territory, which expands over 175 miles (300 kilometers) along the west coast of Vancouver Island. Nuu-chah-nulth means "all along the mountains and sea."

WHERE PEOPLE FEAST is co-authored by the mother-and-daughter team of Dolly (Watts) McRae and Annie Watts. Dolly is a descendant of a long line of high-ranking Chiefs (her Gitk'san Chief name is Lian, meaning "the down of an eagle"). Dolly has learned the customary ways to prepare and serve traditional foods at feasts, celebratory gatherings of indigenous peoples that are a major traditional component of many Native American cultures. Feasts are held to commemorate events such as births, deaths, or totem-pole raisings, during which people exchange gifts, dance, sing, re-enact stories, hear elders speak, and impart culinary knowledge to future generations; many beautiful sacred and ceremonial objects and dance regalia are used in these commemorations.

At the age of ten, Dolly left her family and moved to Port Alberni to attend an Indian residential school. There, she finished twelfth grade, and then got married to Thomas Watts, himself a descendant of a long line of high-ranking Chiefs (his Kwakiutl name is Negye, meaning "Mountain") and a member of the Tseshaht tribe, one of fourteen tribes that make up the Nuu-chah-nulth Nation. Dolly was given the Nuu-chah-nulth name Tuta'he'hlim—meaning "Voice of Thunder." While married, they had three children: Cynthia, Wallace, and Annie.

Through her parents and ancestors, Annie's heritage is truly diverse: she is (through her mother) Gitk'san and Scottish, and (through her father) Nuu-chah-nulth, Kwakiutl, Makah, and English. Before finishing secondary school, Annie worked as a waitress and became interested in becoming a chef. She received a Culinary Arts Degree from

Malaspina College on Vancouver Island, and years later, became interested in obtaining a degree in Computer Science. Around the same time, Dolly moved to Vancouver and attended the University of British Columbia where she earned a Bachelor's degree in Anthropology. She was hired to be a tour guide at the Museum of Anthropology, located on the university grounds. One day, Dolly helped some Native students raise enough money for a field trip by preparing bannock which the students helped fry and then sell; they easily raised enough money to reach their goal. A professor suggested that Dolly set up a table outside the museum and sell bannock on a regular basis. Soon, customers began requesting that Dolly offer soup and salmon with the bannock, and the food cart ensued, which then evolved into a catering business. Dolly had to rent kitchens on the university campus to keep up with demand. Just as it was becoming necessary to find a permanent kitchen for her burgeoning business, a restaurant space became available downtown near Vancouver's busy English Bay, just two blocks from Stanley Park, which became home to their restaurant, Liliget Feast House, the world's only indigenous fine-dining establishment.

WHERE PEOPLE FEAST celebrates Dolly and Annie's twelve years spent running their restaurant ("Liliget" is a Gitk'san word meaning "where people feast"), which was designed by internationally renowned Canadian architect Arthur Erickson. Liliget emulated the interior of a traditional west coast longhouse, with subdued lighting illuminating wooden walkways across pebble floors, contemporary First Nations art on the walls, and long cedar-plank tables with tatami-style cedar-plank benches. Upon opening in 1995, the restaurant was an immediate hit. Annie planned all the menus, cooked part time, and designed all of the promotional materials, taking advantage of the international culinary knowledge she received from the renowned chef instructors while in college and the talented First Nations cooks of Liliget Feast House. Gaining culinary acclaim in Canada and beyond, Dolly won a food competition in Vancouver called the Gold Komochi Konbu Iron Chef Challenge, cooking alongside Japanese chefs on recipes that featured traditional spawn on kelp; she was also recognized with a National Aboriginal Achievement Award for business and commerce. Accolades for the restaurant included a four-star recommendation from the NEW YORK TIMES. WHERE MAGAZINE also voted it Vancouver's "Best Ethnic Cuisine," and Aboriginal Tourism BC awarded Liliget with the "Excellence in Customer Service" Award. The chefs of Liliget Feast House cooked over an alder wood-burning grill, preparing such mouth-watering dishes as Alder-Grilled Marinated Elk (page 16), Sweet Potato Tarts (page 89) with Savory Wild Blueberry Jam (page 171), and Sopalali Mousse (page 142) for dessert for local regulars, out-of-town tourists, and celebrities alike.

WHERE PEOPLE FEAST is a wide-ranging collection of traditional (and not-so-traditional) west coast aboriginal recipes. The first chapter, Wild Game, includes delectable entrées such as Venison Roast with Juniper Berry Rub (page 21), Rabbit Pot Pie (page 29), Chokecherry-Glazed Grouse (page 40), and Wild Buffalo Burgers (page 27). The Seafood chapter showcases recipes for fish and shellfish that run the oceans and rivers of the Pacific Northwest Coast region: salmon, halibut, crab, oysters, clams, scallops, shrimp, and Alaskan Black Cod; oolichan, which populate British Columbia rivers by the millions; and the delicacy herring spawn on kelp. In the Vegetables, Salads & Sides chapter, you'll find recipes for Alder-Grilled Butternut Squash (page 70), Blackberry-Glazed Beets (page 73), the Native interpretation of the classic Caesar salad called Caesar Goes Wild Salad (page 80), and numerous recipes for indigenous wild rice that grows across North America. The chapter Soups & Stocks cooks up mouth-watering soups, stews, chowders, and stocks that use ingredients such as salmon, buffalo, hominy corn, and shiitake mushrooms. Next, the Sauces & Condiments chapter shares Liliget Feast House's special recipes for its popular Dill Sauce (page 125), Raspberry Cranberry Chutney (page 117), and Brown Mushroom Gravy (page 123). Baked Goods & Desserts provides Dolly's claim to fame: Just Like Grandma's Bannock (page 130), a traditional fried bread recipe, as well as many other delicious treats with a First Nations twist. And finally, WHERE PEOPLE FEAST concludes with a unique and insightful chapter, Smoked Foods & Preserves, which provides traditional methods and contemporary recipes for smoking and drying wild game and seafood and preserving berries.

In 2007, Dolly decided to retire and shut down Liliget Feast House to move back to Port Alberni and live with her new husband Ken McRae, who is currently the mayor of Port Alberni. Now that the restaurant has closed its doors, both Dolly and Annie are happy that its legacy can live on in this cookbook.

Berry Picking

A Story by Dolly Watts

I watched my older brothers and sisters get ready to pick berries on the mountain. "We're going to Sta'ghiy'it to pick berries," they whispered in our grandpa's ear. I watched Mom pack their food and blankets and I wished I could go. Two years has passed and it was that time again, time to pick berries.

I had turned seven that summer and I was big enough, I knew. "Please, Mom, I am big now and I will walk fast."

"But what if you get tired or scared when they tell stories at night?"

"I will pick lots of berries and I will go to sleep early, and I will do what Aunty says, and I won't listen to scary stories."

"Alright, get ready!" Mom bundled twelve dried fish and tucked them inside my grey wool blanket and strapped it tightly on my back. I told everyone I was going to Sta'ghiy'it to pick berries.

We climbed up Sta'ghiy'it where I knew shiny blackberries waited. I walked and sometimes ran beside Aunty, her big feet, long legs stepping once, mine twice.

Above, the trees were so high, their tips leaning to tell stories, while beneath my feet was moss and cedar, crimson and soft.

The animals and birds squawked and groaned, male grouse wooed, bears ran, and startled mountain sheep did not transform into humans.

We reached first camp where a lean-to stood waiting to be covered with cedar boughs, and on the ground was blackened wood where a fire once burned.

I undid my bundle and we roasted fish. Hot fat dripped down my chin as I ate. I drank sweet, hot, cedar-flavored tea. The cold mountain air enveloped us, my blanket was wrapped around me, and I watched the flames reach high into the sky as the storytellers' shadows danced while they told stories. I closed my eyes, thinking of huckleberries.

Wild Game

Alder-Grilled Marinated Elk

The Gitk'san people used to trade salmon from the Skeena River for elk with the Okanagan people in central British Columbia. Elk meat is darker and more tender than venison and beef. Serve this dish with sautéed onions, mashed potatoes, vegetables, Brown Mushroom Gravy (page 123), and Savory Wild Blueberry Jam (page 171).

2 elk medallions (5 oz/140 g each) (see note)
4 tbsp onions, chopped
2 cloves garlic, crushed
6 tbsp brown sugar
2 tbsp pineapple juice
2 tbsp Raspberry Balsamic Vinegar (page 118)
2 tsp soy sauce
1½ cups sunflower oil
2 tsp black pepper
1 tsp dried marjoram

In a bowl or dish, marinate elk in remaining ingredients for 2 hours, turning at least 4 times. Remove from marinade and place over an alder wood-burning grill at a high temperature, ensuring flames are close to but not touching meat. Grill elk for 4 minutes on each side or to desired doneness.

Makes 2 servings.

■ Use a stovetop or barbecue grill if you don't have an alder wood-burning grill.

■ Elk can be purchased from gourmet butchers or from online sources.

Alder-Grilled Marinated Venison Chops

Venison is one of the leanest meats available. Deer are abundant in Kitwanga, where Dolly was born and raised for ten years. There are deer trails in people's backyards and Dolly's brothers would go deer hunting, though only when needed. Serve these venison chops with sautéed onions, mashed potatoes, vegetables, Brown Mushroom Gravy (page 123), and Savory Wild Blueberry Jam (page 171).

4 bone-in venison chops (2½ oz/70 g each) (see note)
¼ cup onions, chopped
2 cloves garlic, crushed
¾ cup apple juice
¼ cup Raspberry Balsamic Vinegar (page 118)
¼ cup soy sauce
¾ cup sunflower oil
½ tsp black pepper
½ tsp dried rosemary

In a bowl or dish, marinate venison in remaining ingredients for 2 hours, turning at least 4 times. Remove from marinade and place over an alder wood-burning grill at a high temperature, ensuring flames are close to but not touching meat. Grill for 5 minutes on each side or to desired doneness.

Makes 2 servings.

- Use a stovetop or barbecue grill if you don't have an alder wood-burning grill.

- Venison can be purchased from gourmet butchers or from online sources.

Venison Meatballs

This recipe is an adaptation of Swedish meatballs and a favorite dish of the Gitk'san people. Serve coated with warm Sweet & Tangy Sauce (page 124).

3¼ oz (90 g) ground venison (see note)
3¼ oz (90 g) ground pork
3 tbsp Bannock Breadcrumbs (page 134)
2½ tsp onions, minced
¼ tsp Worcestershire sauce
4 tsp water
Dash of salt
Dash of black pepper

Preheat oven to 375°F (190°C). In a bowl, combine all ingredients and mix thoroughly. Shape into 5 medium-sized meatballs and place in a baking dish, then bake for 15 minutes.

Makes 5 servings.

■ Venison can be purchased from gourmet butchers or from online sources.

Oven-Baked Venison Skewers

A great change-of-pace appetizer.

6 oz (170 g) venison steak, thinly sliced (see note)
3 tbsp Raspberry Zinger Sauce (page 116) (may substitute with barbecue sauce)

Preheat oven to 350°F (180°C). Place venison onto 6-in, pre-soaked wooden skewers (spear through each piece twice). Brush both sides with sauce, place skewers on a baking sheet, and let marinate for 10 minutes. Place in oven and bake for 7 minutes on each side.

Makes 6 servings.

■ Venison can be purchased from gourmet butchers or from online sources.

Wild Shepherd's Pie

This recipe is an adaptation of traditional shepherd's pie, using ground venison and pork instead of beef. It's another favorite dish of the Gitk'san people. Serve with Raspberry Cranberry Chutney (page 117).

2 tbsp butter
2 tbsp sunflower oil
1 lb (450 g) ground venison (see note)
¼ lb (115 g) ground pork
1 cup onions, minced
1 stalk celery, minced
1 clove garlic, minced
Pinch of celery salt
Pinch of white pepper
1 tsp marjoram
½ cup Brown Mushroom Gravy (page 123)
1 tsp Worcestershire sauce
1 cup carrots, minced
1 cup corn kernels
6 cups potatoes, peeled and quartered
¼ cup whole milk
1 tbsp butter
Pinch of white pepper
Pinch of salt

Preheat oven to 350°F (180°C). In a frying pan on high, heat 2 tbsp butter and oil. Sauté venison, pork, onions, celery, garlic, celery salt, pepper, and marjoram for 6 minutes, until onions are translucent. Drain fat. Add gravy, Worcestershire sauce, carrots, and corn. Cover with lid, reduce heat to low, and simmer for 20 minutes, stirring occasionally. In a large pot of salted cold water on high heat, bring potatoes to a boil. Reduce heat to low and simmer for 20 minutes. Drain, then add milk, 1 tbsp butter, pepper, and salt. Mash potatoes until smooth and fluffy. Place meat mixture in the bottom of a buttered 9x13-in (23x33-cm) casserole dish. Spread potato mixture on top and bake for 35 minutes.

Makes 6 servings.

■ Ground venison can be purchased from gourmet butchers or from online sources.

Venison Roast with Juniper Berry Rub

Juniper berries are the deep purple fruit of the juniper bush. Usually sold dried to add flavor to meats and sauces, they have a bitter sweet, pine flavor with a peppery aftertaste. Serve with the Savory Red Currant Jelly (page 128).

1 tbsp dried juniper berries
1 clove garlic
1 tsp cayenne pepper
1 tsp cumin seeds
1 tsp dried onion flakes
1 lb (445 g) venison rump roast (see note)
1 tbsp grapeseed oil
1 cup boiling water

Preheat oven to 350°F (180°C). In a mortar, crush berries, garlic, cayenne pepper, cumin seeds, and onion flakes. Rub the crushed spices onto the roast. In a frying pan on high, heat oil and pan-sear roast on all sides to seal in juices. Place roast in a roasting pan, add boiling water, and roast for 1 hour, basting at least 4 times. Let roast sit for at least 15 minutes before slicing.

Makes 3 servings.

■ Venison can be purchased from gourmet butchers or from online sources.

Venison Stew

Dolly's mom often made this stew for her fifteen-member family. Serve this hearty dish in shallow bowls with crusty bread, or bake dumplings (below) on top of the stew for the last 20 minutes of the cooking time.

2 lbs (900 g) venison stew meat (see note)
¼ cup all-purpose flour
3 tbsp sunflower oil
1 cup tomatoes, peeled, seeded, and chopped
1 cup red wine (Merlot is good)
4 cups Venison Stock (page 107)
Preserved vegetables from Venison Stock (page 107)
1 tsp fresh basil, minced
3 cups Dumpling Batter for Stews (optional) (below)

Preheat oven to 325°F (165°C). In a mixing bowl, coat venison with flour. In a large pot on high, heat oil. Sear meat on all sides for 3 minutes until browned all over. Add tomatoes and deglaze pot with wine. Add stock, vegetables, and basil and bring to a boil. Place stew in a lightly greased casserole dish, cover with lid, and bake for 1 hour. If topping with dumpling batter, pour over stew during the last 20 minutes of cooking time and bake for at least 10 minutes, uncovered, to make sure it browns on top. Cover and bake for an additional 10 minutes at 350°F (180°C) to make sure batter is cooked completely.

Makes 6 servings.

■ Venison stew meat can be purchased from gourmet butchers or from online sources.

DUMPLING BATTER FOR STEWS

This batter is excellent over Venison Stew (above), Rabbit Stew (page 31), Rabbit Pot Pie (page 29), or any other stew, making them heartier.

2 cups milk
1 cup all-vegetable shortening
4 cups all-purpose flour

1 tbsp baking powder
1½ tsp salt

In a bowl, combine all ingredients and mix well.

Makes 3 cups.

Venison Pâté

An exotic alternative to traditional French pâté. For an elegant presentation, serve pâté squeezed onto a lettuce leaf using an icing bag with a large floweret tip, or in an oiled mold. Those who haven't tried venison pâté before will be happily surprised by its rich and unique taste.

2 tbsp butter
½ cup carrots, diced
¼ cup shallots, diced
½ stalk celery, diced
2 cloves garlic, minced
½ tsp salt
1 tsp black pepper
½ tsp dried rosemary
½ tsp dried thyme
½ lb (225 g) venison liver, cut into bite-sized pieces (see note)
Half-and-half cream (on hand)

In a large frying pan on medium-high heat, melt butter. Add remaining ingredients, except for liver and cream, and sauté until vegetables are soft. Add liver and sauté until cooked, then remove pan from heat to cool. In a blender or food processor, blend cooled mixture until smooth. If pâté is too dry, add half-and-half cream, 1 tsp at a time, until moist.

Makes 2 cups.

■ Venison liver can be purchased from gourmet butchers or from online sources.

Venison & Wild Rice Casserole

The aroma of this dish while it is cooking is comforting—a real home-cooking smell.

1½ lbs (675 g) ground venison
½ lb (225 g) ground pork
2 tbsp butter
1 cup onions, minced
¾ cup carrots, minced
½ cup celery, minced
1 cup mushrooms, sliced
3 tbsp all-purpose flour
3 cups Venison Stock (page 107)
2 tbsp teriyaki sauce
3 cups Crème Fraîche (page 127)
2 tsp celery salt
¼ tsp black pepper
6 cups cooked wild rice (see page 83)
½ cup hazelnuts, ground (for garnish)
Fresh parsley (for garnish)

Preheat oven to 350°F (180°C). In a frying pan on high heat, sauté venison and pork until browned all over. Drain fat and set aside. In a large saucepan on high heat, melt butter and sauté onions, carrots, celery, mushrooms, and flour for 5 minutes. Add stock, teriyaki sauce, crème fraîche, celery salt, pepper, cooked rice, and venison-pork mixture. Stir and pour mixture in a lightly greased 9x13-in (23x33-cm) casserole dish and bake for 1 hour, uncovered, stirring occasionally. Garnish with hazelnuts and fresh parsley sprigs.

Makes 10 servings.

Indian Tacos

This is Dolly's version of chili and bannock that is served at most large gatherings of Native Americans.

1 tbsp canola oil
1 lb (455 g) ground venison
1 pkg (40 g) chili seasoning mix
1 tbsp grapeseed oil
½ cup onions, diced
1 stalk celery, diced
2 tbsp green bell peppers, diced
2 tbsp red bell peppers, diced
1 clove garlic, minced
1 can stewed tomatoes (14 oz/414 ml)
1 can red kidney beans (15 oz/440 ml)
5 large prepared Just Like Grandma's Bannock (page 130)
½ cup onions, diced (for garnish)
1 fresh tomato, diced (for garnish)
2 cups lettuce, diced (for garnish)
1¼ cups Cheddar cheese, grated (for garnish)

In a frying pan on high, heat canola oil. Sauté venison until browned all over, then drain fat. Add chili seasoning and stir until mixed, then set aside. In a separate saucepan on high, heat grapeseed oil and sauté onions, celery, peppers, and garlic for 6 minutes. Add stewed tomatoes, beans, and browned venison, stirring continually until heated thoroughly. Heat bannock in the oven. To serve, spread meat mixture on each bannock and garnish with onions, tomatoes, lettuce, and cheese.

Makes 5 servings.

Wild Buffalo Smokies

Buffalo are the largest land mammal in North America; once endangered, their numbers have risen from 1,000 at the turn of the twentieth century to more than 250,000 today. Buffalo meat is naturally sweeter than beef, and has less fat than other meat products. We served these hugely popular buffalo smokies tucked inside bannock slices from our food cart outside the Museum of Anthropology at the University of British Columbia.

2 wild buffalo smokies, sliced diagonally into 3 pieces (see note)
4 tsp Tangy Rhubarb Sauce (page 113)

Preheat oven to 350°F (180°C). In a baking pan, roast smokies for 10 minutes. Serve with Tangy Rhubarb Sauce.

Makes 2 servings.

■ Wild buffalo smokies can be purchased from gourmet butchers or from online sources. You may substitute with any sausages or smokies available.

Wild Buffalo Burgers

Great for any outdoor barbecue party.

1 tbsp sunflower oil
¼ cup onions, diced
1 large egg, beaten
1 clove garlic, minced
2 tbsp Raspberry Balsamic Vinegar (page 118)
1 tsp Dijon mustard
½ tsp dried cilantro (coriander)
½ tsp salt
½ tsp pepper
1 lb (445 g) ground buffalo meat (see note)
4 large Just Like Grandma's Bannock (page 130)
½ cup onion, diced (for garnish)
1 fresh tomato, diced (for garnish)
2 cups lettuce, diced (for garnish)
1¼ cups Cheddar cheese, grated (for garnish)

In a frying pan on medium, heat oil. Add ¼ cup onions and sauté for 6 minutes until softened and remove from heat. In a bowl, combine egg, garlic, vinegar, mustard, cilantro, salt, pepper, ground buffalo, and sautéed onions and mix thoroughly. Shape into 4 patties (½-in/1-cm thick). Over an alder wood-burning grill on high temperature, ensuring flames are close to but not touching meat, cook meat patties for 5 minutes on each side. Cut bannock in half—they are now the "buns." Place meat patties between bannock buns and sprinkle with onions, tomatoes, lettuce, and cheese.

Makes 4 servings.

■ Buffalo meat can be purchased at gourmet butchers or from online sources. You may substitute it with either elk or beef.

■ Use a stovetop or barbecue grill if you don't have an alder wood-burning grill.

Pemmican Canapés

Pemmican is made of wild game, wild berries, and the rendered fat of wild game. Traditionally, bags of pemmican were stored in the stomachs of wild game and rawhide with its fur left on, then sewn up tightly, which kept the pemmican fresh and edible for years. The bags were buried in a cool, dry pit at strategic points on the hunting trail. The pits were lined and covered with birch bark, with rocks piled on top to prevent animals from stealing it.

2 tbsp Mayonnaise (page 126)
2 tsp horseradish sauce
8 lettuce pieces
8 Bannock Crackers (page 135)
8 Pemmican Balls (page 167)

In a bowl, combine mayonnaise and horseradish and mix well. To serve, spread mayonnaise mixture on each cracker, then top with lettuce and then a pemmican ball.

Makes 8 canapés.

Rabbit Pot Pie

Since there is not a large amount of meat on a rabbit, Dolly found a way to add flavor and content to feed more people.

3 lbs (1½ kg) rabbit meat, cut into bite-sized pieces
1 tsp bacon, fried and minced
1½ cups potatoes, cubed
1½ cup carrots, diced
1½ cups onions, diced
1 clove garlic, minced
2 tsp fresh arugula, chopped
1½ tsp celery salt
3 cups boiling water
3 cups Dumpling Batter for Stews (page 22)

Preheat oven to 350°F (180°C). In a large pot on high heat, combine all ingredients except dumpling batter and bring to a boil. Immediately pour into a deep baking dish and bake for 30 minutes, covered. Spoon batter on top of stew and bake for an additional 10 minutes, uncovered, to brown the batter, then cover and bake for an additional 10 minutes to cook the batter completely.

Makes 10 servings.

- Rabbits, either whole or by piece, can be found at gourmet butchers or from online sources.

Oven-Roasted Rabbit with Honey Dijon Dip

In the fall and winter, Dolly's brothers used to snare rabbits, which are everywhere in Kitwanga, the village where she grew up.

1 tbsp canola oil
1 young rabbit (4 lbs/2 kg), with fat, kidneys, and liver removed (see note)
½ tsp dried marjoram
1 tsp bacon, fried and minced
1 tsp garlic, minced
¼ tsp celery salt
¼ tsp black pepper
½ cup Honey Dijon Dip (page 114)

Preheat oven to 325°F (165°C). Use oil to coat a roasting pan, then place rabbit, belly-side down, and sprinkle with marjoram, bacon, garlic, celery salt, and pepper. Roast for 25 minutes. Serve with Honey Dijon Dip.

Makes 3 servings.

■ Young rabbits are available at gourmet butchers or from online sources.

Rabbit Stew

Use the prepared rabbit meat and vegetables from the Rabbit Stock (below) for this wonderful stew. Serve in shallow bowls with crusty bread or bake Dumpling Batter for Stews (page 22) on top for the last 20 minutes of cooking time.

1 cup potatoes, diced
4 cups Rabbit Stock (below)
¼ cup all-purpose flour
½ cup cold water
Preserved meat and vegetables from Rabbit Stock (below)
3 cups Dumpling Batter for Stews (page 22)

Preheat oven to 350°F (180°C). In a large pot on medium heat, combine potatoes and stock and cook until tender. In a large bowl, mix flour and water to make a paste. Add preserved meat and vegetables, cooked potatoes, and mix well, then transfer to a casserole dish or ovenproof pot and cook for 6 minutes. If serving with dumpling batter, spoon batter on top of stew and bake for 10 minutes, uncovered, to brown dumpling batter. Cover and bake for an additional 10 minutes to cook batter completely.

Makes 6 servings.

RABBIT STOCK

3 lbs (1½ kg) rabbit, washed, cut into bite-sized pieces (see note)
2 cups onions, chopped
1 cup celery, chopped
1 cup carrots, chopped
¼ tsp salt
¼ tsp black pepper
Pinch of marjoram
6 cups boiling water

In a stockpot on high heat, bring all ingredients to a boil. Reduce heat to low and simmer for 2 hours.

Makes 4 cups.

■ Rabbits, either whole or by piece, can be found at gourmet butchers or from online sources.

Stuffed Duck Roll

Impress your family and guests with this duck at holiday time instead of turkey. It takes two days, but it's worth the effort. Serve with Brown Mushroom Gravy (page 123), mashed Russet potatoes, vegetables, and Festive Cranberry-Cherry Jam (page 172).

2 whole ducks (2 lb/900 g each) (see note)
10 slices white bread, crusts removed
1 tsp dried marjoram
½ cup onion, diced
½ cup celery, diced
½ tsp salt
½ tsp white pepper
1 cup whipping cream
½ cup egg whites
¼ cup sweetened dried cranberries
Boiling water (enough to cover bottom 1 in of roasting pan)

The day before you wish to serve this, trim off excess fat and remove the wings and pope's nose from the ducks. Cut down the center of the backs. Debone, including legs. Leave meat and skin on one duck. Cut the meat away from the skin of the second duck and place it where the meat is thin or absent on the first duck so there is one flat layer of meat. Set aside to make stuffing. Preheat oven to 350°F (180°C). To make the stuffing, cut bread into small squares and put into a large bowl. Sprinkle marjoram, onions, celery, salt, and pepper over bread and mix gently. Fold in whipping cream gently, then set aside. In another bowl, whip egg whites until they form soft peaks and fold into the bread stuffing. Down the center of the duck meat, layer stuffing with berries. Stuff the legs. Roll meat up around stuffing to form a rolled roast and use skewers to close. Place meat on plastic wrap that measures about 2 feet long. Wrap firmly and tie ends, then firmly wrap in tinfoil. Pour boiling water in roasting pan, place duck roll on top, and roast for 1½ hours in order to remove excess fat. Remove from oven and let cool in the pan then store in refrigerator overnight.

The next day, remove fat from the pan. Roast unwrapped for 1 hour at 350°F (180°C). Cool for 3 hours to allow dressing to set.

Makes 10 servings.

■ You can ask your butcher for help deboning the ducks.

Alder-Grilled Marinated Elk (page 16)

Rabbit Pot Pie (page 29)

Venison Meatballs (page 18)

Stuffed Duck Roll (page 32)

Wild Huckleberry Glazed Duck

Wild huckleberries, which look like dark blueberries, usually ripen in late summer, and taste from tart to sweet, similar to the flavor of blueberries. Traditionally, when the huckleberries ripened in September, women would bring enough food to last them one month in the mountains while they harvested the huckleberries, in case it took that long to collect them. Serve this elegant, slightly sweet duck with mashed Russet potatoes and steamed seasonal vegetables.

1 whole young duck (4 lb/2 kg)
Boiling water (enough to cover
    bottom 1 in of roasting pan)
2 tsp sunflower oil
1 tbsp onions, minced
1 tsp dried marjoram
½ cup red wine (Merlot is good)
2 cups wild huckleberries (see note)

1 cup boiling water
¼ cup honey
¼ cup brown sugar, lightly packed
1 tbsp lemon juice
½ tsp salt
¼ tsp black pepper
1 tbsp cornstarch
¼ cup cold water

The day before you wish to serve this, trim off excess fat and remove neck, gizzard, and kidney from the duck. Tie legs together with butcher string. Preheat oven to 350°F (180°C). Place duck on 2 feet of plastic wrap and firmly wrap the duck and tie plastic wrap at the ends. Then place wrapped duck on 2 feet of tinfoil and firmly wrap again. Pour boiling water into pan, place duck on top, and roast for 1 hour in order to remove excess fat. Remove from oven and let cool. Store in refrigerator overnight.

The next day, preheat oven to 425°F (220°C). Remove tinfoil and plastic wrap from duck and discard fat from pan. In a heavy frying pan on high, heat oil. Sauté onions for 6 minutes, until softened. Add marjoram and stir. Add wine, berries, 1 cup boiling water, honey, sugar, lemon juice, salt, and pepper, mix well and bring to a boil. Reduce heat to medium and simmer for 20 minutes. In a cup, blend cornstarch with cold water and whisk into the glaze. Increase heat to high, bringing glaze to a boil for 2 minutes. Place duck in a deep roasting pan, then drizzle some (not all) glaze over duck. Roast for 15 minutes, then lower oven temperature to 375°F (190°C) and roast for an additional 40 minutes, basting duck occasionally with rest of glaze. When done, the drumstick should separate from duck easily.

Makes 2 or 3 servings.

■ Wild huckleberries can be purchased at specialty markets or from online sources. You may substitute with wild blueberries.

■ You can also use the huckleberry glaze for basting ham, chicken, or pork.

Oven-Roasted Duck

Try this dish instead of roast chicken. Serve with mashed Russet potatoes, vegetables, and Festive Cranberry-Cherry Jam (page 172).

1 whole young duck (4 lb/2 kg) (see note)
1 lemon, cut in half
¼ tsp black pepper
1 tsp fresh rosemary, chopped
2 tsp fresh marjoram, chopped
1 onion, sliced into thin rings

The day before you wish to serve this dish, trim off excess fat and remove neck, gizzard, and kidney from the duck. Tie legs together with butcher string. Preheat oven to 350°F (180°C). Place duck on plastic wrap that measures 2 feet long. Wrap firmly and tie plastic wrap at ends. Then place wrapped duck in 2 feet of tinfoil and firmly wrap again. Roast for 1 hour to cook off extra fat. Remove from oven and let cool. Store in refrigerator overnight.

The next day, preheat oven to 425°F (220°C). Remove tinfoil and plastic wrap from duck and discard fat from pan. Rub skin of duck with lemon. Place duck in a deep baking pan and sprinkle with pepper, rosemary, and marjoram, then top duck with onions. Roast for 15 minutes, then lower oven temperature to 375°F (190°C) and roast for an additional 40 minutes. When done, drumstick should separate from duck easily.

Makes 2 servings.

Alder-Grilled Marinated Duck Breast

The alder wood gives this dish a wonderful smoky quality. Serve with Whipped Sweet Potatoes (page 90), steamed vegetables, and Festive Cranberry-Cherry Jam (page 172).

4 breasts of duck (5 oz/140 g each)
1 cup buttermilk
¼ cup teriyaki sauce
1 cup sunflower oil
¼ cup brown sugar
1 tsp celery salt
1 tsp marjoram
¼ cup Blackberry Syrup (page 177)

In a large bowl, marinate duck in remaining ingredients for 2 hours, turning at least 4 times. Remove from marinade and place over an alder wood-burning grill at a high temperature, ensuring flames are close to but not touching meat. Cook duck for 6 minutes on each side.

Makes 4 servings.

■ Use a stovetop or barbecue grill if you don't have an alder wood-burning grill.

Duck & Wild Rice Casserole

This is a healthy entrée since the duck breast is skinless.

2 tbsp butter
3 cups duck breast, skinless and diced
½ cup onions, diced
½ cup mushrooms, sliced
3 cups cooked wild rice (see page 83)
½ cup ground hazelnuts
3 cups Chicken Stock (page 108)
1 cup Crème Fraîche (page 127)
¼ tsp celery salt
¼ tsp garlic salt
¼ tsp black pepper
¼ tsp cayenne pepper
½ cup Parmesan cheese, freshly grated

Preheat oven to 350°F (180°C). In a large frying pan on medium, melt butter. Sauté duck, onions, and mushrooms, until onions are softened. In a casserole dish, combine duck mixture and remaining ingredients, except for cheese. Cover with a lid or tinfoil and bake for 1½ hours. Remove cover and sprinkle with cheese. Increase oven temperature to 450°F (230°C) and bake uncovered for an additional 5 minutes.

Makes 4 servings.

Alder-Grilled Breast of Pheasant

Dolly's family traditionally used grouse in this recipe, which is plentiful in Kitwanga; however, it's not readily available in Vancouver so at the restaurant, Dolly substituted grouse with pheasant. Pheasant meat is dark but really lean, unlike duck.

2 pheasant breasts (6 oz/170 g each)
2 tsp butter, softened
½ tsp salt
½ tsp black pepper
1 tsp pork fat, minced and heated (to liquefy)
4 tsp Wild Chokecherry Sauce (below)

Preheat oven to 350°F (180°C). Brush pheasant with butter, salt, pepper, and pork fat. Sear both sides on an alder wood-burning grill at high temperature, ensuring flames are close to but not touching meat. Place pheasant in a baking dish and bake for 10 minutes. For each serving, spoon 1 tsp of chokecherry sauce onto a plate and place pheasant on top of sauce, then an additional tsp of sauce on top of pheasant.

Makes 2 servings.

■ Use a stovetop or barbecue grill if you don't have an alder wood-burning grill.

■ Pheasant is available at gourmet butchers or from online sources. If pheasant is unavailable, use grouse, Rock Cornish hen, guinea fowl, or chicken.

WILD CHOKECHERRY SAUCE

1⅓ cups chokecherries
⅔ cup water
⅓ cup white sugar

1 tsp cornstarch
2 tbsp water

In a heavy saucepan over high heat, bring chokecherries, ⅔ cup water, and sugar to a boil. Reduce heat to low and simmer for 20 minutes, then remove from heat and let cool. Pass through a food processor then return to saucepan on high heat and bring to a boil. Whisk in cornstarch and 2 tbsp water. Simmer for 3 minutes, then remove from heat.

Makes 2 cups.

Pheasant in a Blanket

Annie got the idea for this recipe from the classic pig-in-blanket. She uses pastry dough to wrap around each marinated pheasant breast that is filled with cream cheese and Portobello mushrooms.

1 cup buttermilk	4 pheasant breasts (5 oz/140 g each),
¼ cup Blackberry Syrup (page 177)	boneless, skinless, sliced pockets
¼ cup teriyaki sauce	for stuffing (see note)
1 cup sunflower oil	1 cup Portobello mushrooms, sliced
¼ cup brown sugar	2 tbsp onions, diced
1 tsp celery salt	1 tbsp carrots, diced
1 tsp dried marjoram	1 tbsp celery, diced
4 oz cream cheese	Basic Pastry Dough (below)
	Butter (to coat), melted

Preheat oven to 350°F (180°C). In a bowl, combine buttermilk, syrup, teriyaki sauce, oil, sugar, celery salt, and marjoram and stir. Place pheasant in mixture to marinate for 2 hours, turning at least 4 times. To make filling: in a bowl, mix together cream cheese, mushrooms, onions, carrots, and celery, and set aside. Remove pheasant from marinade. Stuff each pheasant breast with filling. On a lightly floured surface, roll Basic Pastry Dough out to ½-in (1½-cm) thick and cut into 2 large rectangles. Place each stuffed pheasant breast on one-half of each rectangle. Brush pastry edges with butter and fold around pheasant breast, making a square bundle. Pinch the edges to seal. Place the bundles on an ungreased roasting pan. Brush remaining butter onto each bundle. Bake for 35 minutes, then cover and continue baking for 10 minutes.

Makes 4 servings.

■ Pheasant can be purchased from gourmet butchers or from online sources.
  If pheasant is unavailable, use grouse, Rock Cornish hen, guinea fowl, or chicken.

BASIC PASTRY DOUGH

5 cups all-purpose flour	1 tsp salt
1 cup shortening	½ cup orange juice
1 cup butter	Ice-cold water (on hand)

In a bowl, combine flour, shortening, butter, and salt and mix well. Add orange juice and mix well. If too dry, add ice-cold water, 1 tbsp at a time, until dough is moist. Refrigerate until needed. Freeze whatever you do not use.

Makes enough pastry dough for 2 pie shells.

Grouse & Wild Rice Casserole

This is an elegant casserole that takes advantage of pre-made soups. Serve with steamed butternut squash.

1 can Cream of Celery Soup (10 oz/300 ml)
1 can Cream of Chicken Soup (10 oz/300 ml)
2/3 cup mushrooms, thinly sliced
1 pkg onion soup mix (1½ oz/45 g)
½ cup cooked wild rice (see page 83)
½ cup cooked white rice
2 lbs (900 g) grouse, cut into bite-sized pieces
¼ tsp salt

Preheat oven to 350°F (180°C). In a large casserole dish, mix all ingredients together, except grouse and salt. Salt grouse pieces and lay on top of mixture. Cover with lid or tinfoil and bake for 1 hour. Remove lid and continue baking for an additional 30 minutes.

Makes 6 servings.

Chokecherry-Glazed Grouse

When Dolly was young, she and other children used to go for walks up a mountain in Kitwanga; when they spotted an unsuspecting grouse, the boys would sneak up on it and club it to bring home for dinner! Grouse has a similar taste to duck. The choke-cherries add a sour, tart flavor and the rosemary adds a savory quality.

1 tsp sunflower oil
2 tbsp onions, diced
1¹/₃ cups chokecherries (see note)
¹/₃ cup golden corn syrup
¹/₂ tsp fresh rosemary, minced
2 lbs (900 g) grouse, cut into bite-sized pieces (see note)

Preheat oven to 350°F (180°C). In a heavy frying pan on high, heat oil and sauté onions for 6 minutes, until softened. Add chokecherries, syrup, and rosemary and bring to a boil, then reduce heat to low and simmer for 15 minutes, stirring occasionally. Place grouse in a roasting pan and coat with some (not all) glaze. Roast for 1¹/₂ hours, brushing grouse with remaining glaze as it roasts.

Makes 6 servings.

- Chokecherries can be purchased from specialty markets or from online sources. You may substitute with cranberries.

- Grouse can be purchased from gourmet butcher or from online sources. If grouse is unavailable, you may use pheasant, Rock Cornish hen, guinea fowl, or chicken.

Seafood

Oven-Poached Smoked Alaskan Black Cod

Alaskan black cod is also known as sablefish. It has a rich and delicate flavor and light buttery texture. The Gitk'san live inland, and the young people were often encouraged to marry someone from the coast; Dolly's sister Camilla did this and as a result Dolly and her family got to eat Alaskan black cod often. Serve with Wild Rice Medley (page 84), steamed vegetables, Sweet Raspberry Onions (page 75), Dill Sauce (page 125), and a lemon wedge.

1 tbsp all-purpose flour
¼ tsp salt
¼ tsp black pepper
¼ tsp allspice
1 egg, beaten
1 tbsp whipping cream
2 tbsp corn grits
¼ tsp dried parsley
2 Smoked Alaskan black cod fillets (5 oz/140 g each) (see note)
¾ cup boiling water

Preheat oven to 500°F (260°C). In a small bowl, mix flour, salt, pepper, and allspice. In another small bowl, mix egg and whipping cream. In a third bowl, mix corn grits and parsley. Dip flesh side of the cod fillets in each mixture. In a small baking dish, place fish skin-side down in the water and poach in oven for 10 minutes.

Makes 2 servings.

■ Smoked Alaskan black cod is available at specialty seafood markets or from online sources.

Baked Halibut

All the men in our family were ocean fishermen who fished off the coast of British Columbia between the Queen Charlotte Islands and the mainland, which meant we ate halibut at least once a week during the summer. Serve with Wild Rice Medley (page 84), vegetables, and Dill Sauce (page 125).

2 halibut steaks or fillets (5 oz/140 g each)
¼ cup onions, sliced into thin rings
½ tsp salt
½ tsp white pepper
½ tsp dried basil
2 tsp lemon juice

Preheat oven to 500°F (260°C). In a small baking dish, place halibut, then top with remaining ingredients. Bake for 10 minutes.

Makes 2 servings.

■ This recipe also works well with wild salmon steaks or fillets instead of halibut.

Hot Lemon Butter Halibut

The lemon and butter gives life to this halibut dish. Serve with the Wild Rice Medley (page 84), steamed vegetables, and Dill Sauce (page 125).

2 halibut steaks or fillets (5 oz/140 g each)
2 tsp lemon juice
2 tbsp butter, melted
½ tsp dried dill weed
¼ tsp salt
¼ tsp black pepper

Preheat oven to 500°F (260°C). In a baking dish, place halibut and bake for 10 minutes. In a bowl, combine all remaining ingredients and whisk together. Remove halibut from oven and drizzle mixture over top.

Makes 2 servings.

Grandma's Spicy Crabcakes

Dungeness crab is found in British Columbia fishing areas including the Skeena River estuary and the waters off Tofino on the west coast of Vancouver Island, where the Ahousat people fish and used to drop off sacks full of crabs for Annie's grandma to use for her famous spicy crabcakes. Serve with Spicy Corn Salsa (page 120).

1 cup cooked fresh crabmeat, diced
1 tbsp cooked corn kernels
2 tsp jalapeño chili peppers, stemmed, seeded, and minced
2 tbsp green onions, diced
1 clove garlic, minced
2 tbsp Havarti cheese, grated
¼ cup Bannock Breadcrumbs (page 134)
2 tsp teriyaki sauce
Yolks of 2 large eggs
2 tbsp whipping cream, lightly whipped
2 tbsp corn oil
1 tbsp butter, softened
¼ tsp dried dill weed
¼ tsp dry mustard
¼ tsp celery salt
¼ tsp cayenne pepper
Whites of 2 large eggs
2 tbsp all-purpose flour
2 tbsp Bannock Breadcrumbs (page 134)

Preheat oven to 350°F (180°C). Cover a baking sheet with non-stick cooking spray. In a bowl, combine all ingredients except the egg whites, flour, and 2 tbsp breadcrumbs. In a separate stainless steel bowl, whip egg whites until they form soft peaks, then fold into crab mixture. Let stand for 5 minutes to set. Shape mixture into 12 rounds (1 in/2½ cm diameter), then sprinkle with flour and 2 tbsp breadcrumbs. Bake for 20 minutes. Remove from oven and let cool before serving.

Makes 12 cakes.

Crab Mousse

This is great as an appetizer or for any buffet. Serve with small Just Like Grandma's Bannock (page 130), cut into halves.

3 envelopes unflavored gelatin (¼ oz/7 g each)
¼ cup Salmon Stock (page 106)
2 cups fresh cooked crabmeat, diced
²/₃ cup Mayonnaise (page 126)
²/₃ cup sour cream
2 tbsp lemon juice
½ tsp teriyaki sauce
¼ tsp celery salt
¼ tsp cayenne pepper
½ tsp dried dill weed
¼ cup green onions, diced
Indian candy (for garnish) (see note)
Leafy lettuce leaves (for garnish)
Lemon wedges (for garnish)

In a saucepan on high heat, melt gelatin into stock. In a food processor on high speed, combine remaining ingredients, except garnishes, and process until mixture is smooth. Cover mousse mold with non-stick cooking spray. Pour mixture inside mold and refrigerate for 4 hours. Remove from refrigerator and carefully transfer mousse out of mold onto a platter garnished with Indian candy, lettuce leaves, and lemon wedges.

Makes 4 cups.

■ Indian candy is a delicious treat of smoked salmon sweetened with molasses or brown sugar. It can be purchased anywhere salmon or smoked salmon is sold.

Crab & Feta Melt

This is an elegant grilled sandwich great for any occasion.

1 cup cooked fresh crabmeat, diced
¼ cup cooked corn kernels
4 tbsp feta cheese, crumbled
2 tbsp Mayonnaise (page 126)
2 tsp onions, diced
2 tsp celery, diced
¼ tsp dried dill weed
½ tsp garlic salt
¼ tsp black pepper
2 tbsp butter, at room temperature
8 slices sourdough bread
¾ cup Cheddar cheese, grated

In a bowl, stir together all ingredients except butter, bread, and Cheddar cheese, then set aside. Butter one side of 4 bread slices. In a frying pan on medium heat, place 4 slices buttered-side down. Spread crab mixture evenly over slices in frying pan then add a layer of Cheddar cheese. Place remaining 4 bread slices on top of mixture, then butter them. Cover pan with lid and grill sandwiches for 2 minutes on each side.

Makes 4 servings.

Pacific Macaroni & Cheese

Surprise your guests with this exquisite casserole that includes fresh crabmeat, freshly grated Parmesan cheese, and Bannock Breadcrumbs (page 134).

3 tbsp butter
2 tsp onions, diced
2 tsp celery, diced
3 tbsp flour
½ tsp salt
¼ tsp black pepper
1½ cups Crème Fraîche (page 127)
2 cups cooked fresh crabmeat, diced
1 cup sharp Cheddar cheese, grated
½ cup cooked peas
2 cups cooked elbow macaroni
½ cup Bannock Breadcrumbs (page 134)
2 tbsp Parmesan cheese, freshly grated

Preheat oven to 350°F (180°C). In a frying pan on medium heat, melt butter and sauté onions and celery for 5 minutes. Blend in flour, salt, and pepper, then add crème fraîche. Reduce heat to low to simmer for 5 minutes, stirring continually. Fold in crabmeat, Cheddar cheese, peas, and macaroni. Pour into a lightly greased casserole dish, then sprinkle with breadcrumbs and Parmesan cheese. Bake for 25 minutes.

Makes 6 servings.

Crabmeat Salad

A refreshing salad to bring to a picnic or serve for lunch.

1 cup cooked fresh crabmeat, diced
¼ cup onions, minced
¼ cup carrots, diced
¼ cup celery, diced
½ cup cherry tomatoes, quartered
3 tbsp Raspberry Zinger Sauce (page 116)
1 tsp dried dill weed
½ tsp celery salt
½ tsp cayenne pepper
4 large lettuce leaves

In a bowl, combine all ingredients except lettuce and mix well. Cover and refrigerate for 30 minutes. For each serving, place a lettuce leaf on a plate and top with crabmeat mixture.

Makes 4 servings.

Clam Fritters

Dolly loves corn fritters; one day, she tried using clams instead of corn, and voilà — clam fritters! Manila clams were introduced to British Columbia in 1930 when Japanese oyster seeds were imported, and are found in the ocean when it's above the half-tide level. Using canned clams will avoid having to prepare them in the shell, and you can use the nectar that comes with it. Serve with Sweet & Tangy Sauce (page 124).

1¼ cups all-purpose flour
½ tsp baking powder
½ tsp salt
¼ tsp cardamom powder
¼ cup onions, diced
1 stalk celery, diced
1 5-oz (149-ml) can whole baby clams with nectar
Yolk of 1 large egg
White of 1 large egg, lightly beaten
Canola oil (for deep frying)

In a large bowl, combine all ingredients except egg white and oil and mix well, then set aside. In a second bowl, beat egg white until it forms soft peaks, then fold into batter. Heat canola oil in a deep fryer set to 350°F (180°C). Using a small ice cream scoop, carefully drop batter into hot oil and deep fry for 5 minutes until light brown. Place cooked fritters on paper towel to blot excess oil.

Makes 12 fritters.

Shrimp Fritters

Annie created this recipe to take advantage of the abundance of shrimp in the Pacific Northwest. Serve as an appetizer, or use this recipe for dessert fritters by substituting the shrimp with sliced fruit like apples or bananas.

1¼ cups all-purpose flour
½ tsp baking powder
½ tsp salt
½ cup whole milk
1 tsp canola oil
Yolks of 2 large eggs
6 oz (170 g) jumbo shrimp, peeled, deveined, and chopped
Whites of 2 large eggs, lightly beaten
Canola oil (for deep frying)

In a bowl, combine flour, baking powder, salt, milk, 1 tsp oil, egg yolks, and shrimp, mix well, then set aside. In a second bowl, beat egg whites until they form soft peaks, then fold into batter. Heat canola oil in a deep fryer set to 350°F (180°C). Use a small ice cream scoop to carefully drop batter into hot oil. Deep fry for 5 minutes until lightly brown. Place cooked fritters on paper towel to blot excess oil.

Makes 12 fritters.

Deep-Fried Oysters

A great appetizer or light meal; this batter is similar to the one used for the Deep-Fried Oolichan (page 67).

1 cup all-purpose flour
1 tsp baking powder
½ tsp baking soda
½ tsp cornstarch
2 tbsp butter
Yolks of 2 large eggs
½ tsp salt
1 cup half-and-half cream
Canola oil (for deep frying)
6 large fresh oysters, shucked, baked for 10 minutes in nectar, then drained
2 tbsp all-purpose flour

In a large bowl, combine 1 cup flour, baking powder, baking soda, cornstarch, butter, egg yolks, salt, and cream, and mix well. Heat canola oil in a deep fryer set to 375°F (190°C). Dip oysters in 2 tbsp flour, then dip in prepared batter. Drop carefully into hot oil and deep fry for 5 minutes until golden brown. Place fried oysters on paper towel to blot excess oil.

Makes 2 servings.

■ You may substitute the oysters with large scallops, chopped cauliflower, onion slices, or zucchini slices.

Alder-Grilled Oysters

A wonderful way to prepare fresh oysters. Serve with Wild Rice Medley (page 84) and Dill Sauce (page 125).

12 large fresh oysters, shucked, reserve the nectar

Preheat oven to 350°F (180°C). In a pan, bake oysters with nectar for 20 minutes. Remove from oven and let cool. Over an alder wood-burning grill, cook oysters for 4 minutes on each side.

Makes 6 servings.

■ Use a stovetop or barbecue if you don't have an alder wood-burning grill.

Bounty of the Sea

This bouillabaisse is indigenous to the coastal peoples and is a great way to try many seafood items at once. Use fresh ingredients wherever possible.

4 cups water
2 salmon pieces (2 oz/60 g each)
2 halibut pieces (2 oz/60 g each)
4 live mussels, cleaned (see note)
4 live clams, cleaned (see note)
4 large scallops
4 large prawns
4 cups Basil & Garlic Tomato Sauce (page 122), heated
Dried seaweed (for garnish)

In a saucepan on high heat, boil water then add seafood. Poach for 5 minutes (careful not to overcook), then strain. In a large serving dish, pour tomato sauce over seafood, and sprinkle with seaweed.

Makes 2 servings.

■ When preparing live mussels and clams, discard any that are opened. After cooking, discard any that remain closed.

Butter Pecan Scallops over Arugula

This recipe makes a great appetizer. The pecans add a lovely crisp coating. Annie says that although this is not a traditional dish, it still tastes good!

2 tbsp sunflower oil
4 tsp butter
4 large scallops, rinsed with cold water and patted dry
8 capers
4 tbsp golden corn syrup
4 tbsp Worcestershire sauce
½ tsp cayenne pepper
1 tsp pecans, ground
2 cups arugula leaves, washed and torn

In a frying pan on medium, heat oil and butter. Sauté scallops, capers, syrup, sauce, and pepper for 2 minutes on each side. Remove from heat and sprinkle scallops with pecans. For each serving, place arugula leaves on a plate and top with scallop mixture.

Makes 2 servings.

Smoked Salmon Pasta

The smoked salmon gives this creamy spaghettini dish a wonderful texture. Serve with the Caesar Goes Wild Salad (page 80) for a complete meal.

1½ cups Crème Fraîche (page 127)
1 tbsp butter
1 tsp onions, diced
1 tsp cucumbers, diced
1 tbsp all-purpose flour
1 tsp fresh basil, minced
1 tsp fresh dill, minced
¼ tsp celery salt
¼ tsp white pepper
1 Half-Smoked Salmon (8 oz/225 g) (see note)
½ cup boiling water
2 cups cooked spaghettini

Preheat oven to 500°F (260°C). In a heavy saucepan on high heat, whisk together all ingredients, except for salmon, water, and pasta, and bring to a boil. Stir constantly until sauce thickens. In a baking pan, place salmon and water and poach in oven for 10 minutes. Remove from oven then remove salmon skin, flake salmon into pieces, and blend into sauce. Add sauce to pasta and mix well.

Makes 5 servings.

■ See page 165 for how to make half-smoked salmon; otherwise you can purchase it at specialty or seafood markets.

Poached Half-Smoked Wild Salmon

This recipe is a favorite dish of the Tseshaht people who live on the west coast of Vancouver Island. Serve with the Wild Rice Medley (page 84), vegetables, Sweet Raspberry Onions (page 75), and Dill Sauce (page 125) .

2 Half-Smoked Wild Salmon fillets (5 oz/140 g each) (see note)
1/3 tsp lemon zest
1/3 tsp lime zest
1/3 tsp orange zest
3/4 cup boiling water

Preheat oven to 500°F (260°C). In a baking pan, place salmon and zests in boiling water. Poach in oven for 10 minutes. Remove zests from water to serve on top of salmon.

Makes 2 servings.

■ See page 165 for how to make half-smoked salmon; otherwise you can purchase it at specialty or seafood markets.

Smoked Salmon Mousse

This mousse is great to serve at any event or dinner party, with plenty of Just Like Grandma's Bannock (page 130) cut in halves.

1½ tbsp unflavored gelatin
¼ cup cooking wine (sherry is good)
1½ cups canned salmon, de-boned
1 cup smoked salmon
2/3 cup sour cream
2/3 cup Mayonnaise (page 126)
2 tsp horseradish sauce
Dash of Worcestershire sauce
Dash of dried dill weed
Dash of salt
Dash of black pepper
Indian candy (for garnish) (see note)
Leafy lettuce (for garnish)
Lemon wedges (for garnish)

In the top portion of a double boiler on high heat, combine gelatin and wine and cook for 2 minutes, stirring continually. In a blender, combine remaining ingredients, except for garnishes, and blend for 1 minute, then add to gelatin mixture and mix well. Cover a mousse mold with non-stick cooking spray. Pour mixture into mold and refrigerate for 4 hours until firm. Remove from refrigerator and carefully transfer the mousse out of mold onto a platter that is garnished with Indian candy, leafy lettuce, and lemon wedges.

Makes 4 cups.

■ Indian candy is a delicious treat of smoked salmon sweetened with molasses or brown sugar. It can be purchased where smoked salmon is sold.

Alder-Grilled Marinated Wild Salmon

The major spawning runs of sockeye salmon in British Columbia are found in the watersheds that drain off the Fraser, Skeena, and Nass rivers. Wild salmon is widely available in regular or specialty markets. Serve this dish with Wild Rice Medley (page 84), vegetables, and Dill Sauce (page 125).

2 wild salmon fillets (5 oz/140 g each)
¼ cup onions, chopped
6 tbsp brown sugar
6 tbsp Raspberry Balsamic Vinegar (page 118)
¼ cup soy sauce
3 tbsp lemon juice
3 tbsp pineapple juice
½ tsp black pepper
½ tsp dried dill weed

In a bowl, marinate salmon in all remaining ingredients for up to 2 hours, turning at least 4 times. Remove salmon from marinade. Over an alder wood-burning grill at high temperature, ensuring flames are close to but do not touch salmon, cook salmon flesh-side down for 5 minutes. Flip and grill on skin side for an additional 5 minutes.

Makes 2 servings.

■ Use a stovetop or barbecue grill if you don't have an alder wood-burning grill.

Baked Stuffed Wild Salmon

Serve this elegant stuffed salmon as an alternative to turkey, with the Wild Rice Medley (page 84) and Dill Sauce (page 125).

10 slices white bread, cut into bite-sized pieces
¼ cup sweetened dried apples, diced
1 cup Crème Fraîche (page 127)
¼ cup Mayonnaise (page 126)
1 tbsp white corn syrup
½ cup onions, minced
¼ cup carrots, minced
¼ cup celery, diced
1 clove garlic, minced
1 tbsp lemon zest
2 tsp dried dill weed
1 tsp lemon thyme
1 large wild salmon (10 lb/4½ kg), gutted and cleaned with cold water

Preheat oven to 350°F (180°C). In a bowl, combine all ingredients, except for salmon, and mix well. On a lightly greased baking sheet, place salmon and stuff with prepared mixture. Grease a large piece of tinfoil, wrap salmon, and bake for 45 minutes.

Makes 10 servings.

Fast Fish Hash

This dish, which uses salmon left over from preparing stock, makes for a quick and tasty lunch. Serve with Raspberry Zinger Sauce (page 116).

2 tbsp canola oil
½ cup onions, diced
2 cups potatoes, peeled and cut into bite-sized pieces
3 cups salmon pieces preserved from making Salmon Stock (see page 106)
¼ tsp celery salt
¼ tsp white pepper
Pinch of dried basil

In a frying pan on medium, heat oil. Add onions and potatoes and sauté until lightly brown, then add salmon. Cook until salmon is heated through. Sprinkle with celery salt, pepper, and basil.

Makes 2 servings.

Alder-Grilled Salmon Belly Bits

Salmon bellies are usually removed from the fish before processing because they are too fatty and if left on, the salmon may turn rancid during the drying or storing process. But salmon bellies are delicious on their own, usually boiled fresh or half-smoked, and their oils can be used instead of butter for baked potatoes. Serve as a snack over braised lettuce and garnish with a lemon wedge and a sprig of fresh parsley, or serve as a meal with potatoes, vegetables, and Dill Sauce (page 125).

1 tbsp Raspberry Balsamic Vinegar (page 118)
1 tsp salt
1 tsp freshly ground pepper
Salmon belly strips from ½ whole wild salmon, cut into 1-in (2½-cm) cubes (see note)

In a small bowl, combine vinegar, salt, and pepper. Brush salmon belly pieces with vinegar mixture. Grill salmon pieces over an alder wood-burning grill at high temperature, ensuring flames are close to but do not touch salmon, flesh-side down, for 2 minutes on each side.

Makes 2 servings.

■ Salmon bellies can be purchased at your local or specialty seafood market or from online sources. You may need to pre-order them.

Stir Fry Herring Spawn on Kelp

This recipe won Dolly the "Iron Chef" award at the BC Gold Komochi Konbu Chefs' Challenge. Herring spawn their eggs on anything that is in their way, such as sea grass or kelp. To gather spawn, fishermen lower cedar or Pacific Hemlock branches into the ocean at low tide; when the tide rises, herring spawn on the tree branches. Before the tide recedes, fishermen pull the branches from the water and carefully remove the spawn. Herring roe has a mild, creamy, salty taste, and its texture is between crispy and spongy; it can be eaten fresh or cooked. If roe is salted, soak in cold running water for one day before using to remove excess salt.

1 tbsp canola oil
1 slice bacon, diced
½ cup celery, angle sliced
3 center stalks of bok choy, cut into strips
3 green onions, sliced
¼ green bell pepper, slivered
8 oz (225 g) spawn on kelp, cut into strips (see notes)
2 tbsp soy sauce

In a frying pan on high, heat oil and sauté bacon. Add celery, bok choy, green onions, and peppers, and continue to sauté until cooked. Add spawn on kelp and continue to sauté for 3 minutes. Sprinkle with soy sauce.

Makes 4 servings.

- Herring spawn on kelp is about ½-in (1¼-cm) thick and comes in different sizes. You may purchase it from specialty seafood markets or from online sources.

- Do not overcook the spawn, as it will harden and taste chalky.

Garlic Butter Spawn on Kelp

This dish also earned Dolly the "Iron Chef" honor. In Japan, herring spawn on kelp is a delicacy called Komochi Konbu.

2 tbsp unsalted butter
2 cloves garlic, minced
8 oz (225 g) spawn on kelp, cut into strips (see notes)

In a frying pan on medium, heat butter and sauté garlic for 2 minutes. Add spawn on kelp and heat for 3 minutes.

Makes 4 servings.

■ Herring spawn on kelp is about ½-in (1¼-cm) thick and comes in different sizes. It can be bought from specialty seafood markets or from online sources.

■ Do not overcook the spawn, as it will harden and taste chalky.

Oven-Poached Smoked Alaskan Black Cod (page 42)

Bounty of the Sea (page 54)

Alder-Grilled Marinated Wild Salmon (page 59) on Wild Rice (page 83)

Stir Fry Herring Spawn on Kelp (page 63)

Lemon Smoked Oolichan on Butter Lettuce

Oolichan are a small, silvery fish found along the Pacific Coast between Alaska and California, and are most similar in taste and texture to anchovies. There are old, well-traveled "grease trails" through the coastal mountains that lead to the rivers where the oolichan arrive in early April. Their prized oil is extracted and is a valuable trade commodity for the coastal people, for both cooking and fuel.

6 smoked oolichan (see note)
2 cups boiling water
1 tbsp lemon juice
¼ cup white sugar
1 tsp mustard seed
½ tsp black pepper

½ tsp allspice
1 tsp dried dill weed
¾ cup onions, diced
¾ cup carrots, julienned
4 butter lettuce leaves

In a frying pan on high heat, poach oolichan in boiling water for 5 minutes. Debone and cut oolichan into long thin pieces. In a small frying pan on medium heat, combine lemon juice, sugar, mustard seed, pepper, allspice, and dill weed and bring to a boil, stirring frequently. Remove from heat and let cool. In a wide-mouth Mason jar, layer onions, carrots, and oolichan pieces. Repeat layers until all ingredients are used. Pour cooled lemon juice liquid over oolichan mixture. Cover and refrigerate for at least 24 hours, or up to two weeks. For each serving, place two leaves of butter lettuce end to end on each plate. Place carrots on one leaf and onions on the other. Place 3 pieces of oolichan on top.

Makes 2 servings.

■ Smoked oolichan can be bought from specialty seafood markets or from online sources. Or, to make your own: prepare for smoking by piercing whole oolichan through the gills and mouth and thread onto cedar bark ropes that are tied between 2 upright poles in the open air on a sunny day. Build a slow-burning alder wood fire nearby to keep insects away and impart a smoky flavor. Wtih dry weather and steady smoke, oolichan can be properly smoked in 5 days. Store in a sealed container in the freezer.

Baked Fresh Oolichan

Serve this simple yet unique dish with with rice or potatoes.

6 fresh oolichan, heads removed (see note)
2 tbsp all-purpose flour
¼ tsp salt
¼ tsp black pepper

Preheat oven to 500°F (260°C). Dust oolichan with flour, salt, and pepper, then place on a baking sheet to bake for 5 minutes.

Makes 2 servings.

■ Oolichan can be bought from specialty fishmongers or from online sources. You may substitute with any small and oily fish such as anchovies or sardines.

Deep-Fried Oolichan

Although Dolly used to drive out to the fishermen's docks in Richmond outside Vancouver looking for "Fresh Oolichan Sold Here" signs, you may have an easier time purchasing them from specialty seafood markets or from online sources. (You may substitute the oolichan with any small and oily fish such as anchovies or sardines.) Serve as a snack or as a meal with the Wild Rice Salad (page 84), vegetables, and Raspberry Zinger Sauce (page 116).

1 cup all-purpose flour
1 tsp baking powder
½ tsp baking soda
2 tsp cornstarch
Yolks of 2 large eggs
1 tsp salt
1 cup half-and-half cream
6 fresh oolichan, heads removed (see note)
2 tbsp all-purpose flour

Preheat deep fryer to 375°F (190°C). In a large bowl, combine flour, baking powder, baking soda, cornstarch, egg yolks, salt, and cream. Dip oolichan in 2 tbsp flour, then dip in prepared batter, and deep fry for 5 minutes until golden brown. Place fried oolichan on a paper towel to blot excess oil.

Makes 2 servings.

■ You may eat the bones or pick them out; the backbones come off easily.

Vegetables, Salads & Sides

Alder-Grilled Butternut Squash

Serve this smoky side dish with the Alder-Grilled Marinated Elk (page 16). For variety, use a cookie cutter to create fun shapes before marinating and grilling.

2 tsp sunflower oil
½ tsp celery salt
½ tsp allspice
1 tsp brown sugar
1½ cups butternut squash, cut into ½-in (1-cm) thick rounds

In a blender or food processor on high, combine oil, celery salt, allspice, and sugar and blend until emulsified. Cover squash rounds with mixture and cook over an alder wood-burning grill at high temperature, ensuring flames are close to but not touching squash, for 4 minutes on each side.

Makes 2 servings.

■ Use a stovetop or barbecue grill if you don't have an alder wood-burning grill.

Zucchini & Corn Medley

A great side dish, especially if you serve immediately and do not overcook.

1 tbsp corn oil
¼ cup onions, minced
1 clove garlic, minced
2 cups corn kernels
4 cups zucchini, chopped into bite-sized pieces
Pinch of dried cilantro (coriander)
Pinch of celery salt
Pinch of white pepper
¼ cup cold water

In a saucepan on medium, heat oil. Sauté onions, garlic, and corn for 10 minutes until onions are softened. Add remaining ingredients and mix. Reduce heat to low, cover with lid, and let simmer until vegetables are tender, about 15 minutes.

Makes 5 servings.

Parsnip & Yam Medley

Yams are orange-fleshed sweet potatoes, a starchy edible root; they originated in West Africa and Asia and are imported from the Caribbean. Parsnips grow best in colder climates and are well known for their distinct, semi-sweet flavor and aroma when cooked.

3 cups parsnips, peeled and julienned
2 cups yams, peeled and julienned
1 tbsp lemon juice
1 tbsp maple syrup
¼ tsp ground nutmeg
1½ tbsp ground hazelnuts, toasted (for garnish)

In a pot of boiling water on high heat, cook parsnips and yams for 7 minutes until soft but not mushy, then remove from heat and drain. In a small bowl, combine lemon juice, maple syrup, and nutmeg and whisk together, then pour over cooked vegetables. Garnish with hazelnuts.

Makes 5 servings.

Blackberry-Glazed Beets

A slightly sweet condiment that uses beets. Nuu-chah-nulth people of the Northwest Coast tribes on Vancouver Island call blackberries "chismapt"—a trailing, vine-like berry that grows in rocky, dry, open sites. Bush blackberries resemble red raspberry plants, which are called "hisshitlampt." Serve this delicious garnish with hearty dishes; you can also combine it with the Sweet & Tangy Purple Cabbage (page 74).

1½ cups beets, chopped into bite-sized pieces
2 cups boiling water
¼ cup onions, sliced into thin rings
¼ cup Blackberry Vinegar (page 115)
¼ cup Blackberry Syrup (page 177)

In a saucepan on high heat, bring beets and water to a boil. Continue boiling for 20 minutes. Strain and let cool. In a bowl, combine onions and beets and set aside. In a saucepan on high heat, combine vinegar and syrup, bring to a boil, then pour over beets and onions and mix. Remove from heat and let cool. Stir gently and serve, or store in a sealed container in refrigerator, remembering to stir occasionally.

Makes 1½ cups.

Sweet & Tangy Purple Cabbage

Serve this pickle-like cabbage as a garnish for all wild game and seafood entrées.

½ cup purple cabbage, diced
⅛ cup sweetened dried cranberries
¼ cup Raspberry Vinegar (page 118)
3 tbsp Raspberry Syrup (page 176)

In a bowl, combine cabbage and cranberries and set aside. In a saucepan on high heat, combine vinegar and syrup and bring to a boil, then pour over cabbage and cranberries and mix well. Allow mixture to cool and serve, or store in a sealed container in the refrigerator.

Makes ½ cup.

Sweet Raspberry Onions

This sweet red onion condiment can be used to garnish the Poached Half-Smoked Salmon (page 57) or Oven-Poached Alaskan Black Cod (page 42).

½ cup Raspberry Vinegar (page 118)
⅓ cup Raspberry Syrup (page 176)
½ tsp celery salt
½ tsp white pepper
Dash of garlic salt
2 cups red onions, sliced into thin rings

In a saucepan on high heat, combine vinegar, syrup, celery salt, pepper, and garlic salt and bring to a boil. Add onions and boil for an additional 5 minutes. Remove from heat and let cool, then serve or store in a sealed container in the refrigerator.

Makes 1 cup.

Vegetarian Mousse

Serve this vegetarian spread with crackers, slices of baguette, or Just Like Grandma's Bannock (page 130).

1 tbsp agar agar flakes (see note)
2 tbsp white wine (Chardonnay is good)
6 tbsp boiling water
1 tbsp sweet bell peppers (red, green, or yellow), minced
1 tbsp broccoli, minced
1 tbsp cauliflower, minced
2½ tsp wild mushrooms, sliced
2½ tsp purple onions, diced
4 tsp sour cream
4 tsp Mayonnaise (page 126)
½ tsp canola oil
Dash of dried basil
Dash of dried thyme
Dash of dried rosemary

In a saucepan on medium heat, combine agar agar flakes, wine, and boiling water, stirring constantly for 2 minutes, until flakes dissolve. Remove from heat and pour into a blender or food processor, then combine remaining ingredients. Pulse until well blended. Cover the inside of a mold with non-stick cooking spray, then fill with mixture. Refrigerate for 4 hours. To remove mousse from mold, loosen edges with a sharp knife. Once loosened, place upside down on a platter. Place a hot cloth on top of mold until the mousse is released. Store in refrigerator until ready to serve.

Makes 5 servings.

■ Agar agar is a vegetarian gelatin made from seaweed. It can be purchased in the baking or Asian section of grocery stores. You can use regular gelatin in this recipe; just be aware that it contains animal products.

Roasted Yam & Feta Salad

This recipe can be served warm as a main dish and any leftovers can be stored in the freezer.

2 large yams, skins on, cut into bite-sized pieces
½ cup onions, thinly sliced
2 tsp brown sugar
¼ tsp garlic salt
2 tbsp grapeseed oil
4 oz (115 g) feta cheese, cut into bite-sized pieces
1 tbsp lemon juice

Preheat oven to 400°F (200°C). On a baking sheet, toss yams, onions, sugar, garlic salt, and oil. Roast for 20 minutes, turn yams over and roast for an additional 20 minutes. Remove from oven, sprinkle with cheese and lemon juice, and toss well.

Makes 4 servings.

Roasted New Potato Salad

This recipe takes advantage of new potatoes when they are widely available and is a tasty addition to picnics or family gatherings.

1¼ lbs (570 g) new potatoes, skins on, cut into bite-sized pieces
1½ tbsp grapeseed oil
¼ tsp garlic salt
¼ cup sundried tomatoes
½ tsp Raspberry Vinegar (page 118)
½ tsp garlic, minced
¼ tsp dried basil
¼ tsp dried cilantro (coriander)

Preheat oven to 400°F (200°C). In a baking dish, toss potatoes with oil and garlic salt. Cover with lid and roast for 55 minutes. In a blender or food processor on high, combine tomatoes, vinegar, garlic, basil, and cilantro and blend until emulsified. Add mixture to potatoes and toss well.

Makes 4 servings.

Wildman Salad with Blackberry Poppy Seed Dressing

Serve this simple, tangy salad with wild salmon dishes.

4 cups spinach, washed and torn
¼ cup red onions, cut into thin rings
3 tbsp Blackberry Poppy Seed Dressing (below)

In a large salad bowl, combine spinach, onions, and dressing, and toss well.

Makes 2 servings.

BLACKBERRY POPPY SEED DRESSING

1 cup Blackberry Syrup (page 177)
½ cup Blackberry Vinegar (page 115)
1 tbsp poppy seeds
1 cup sunflower oil
1 tbsp red onions, minced
1 tsp nutmeg
2 tbsp sun-dried tomatoes, chopped

In a blender or food processor on high, combine all ingredients and blend until emulsified. Store leftovers in a sealed container in the refrigerator.

Makes 2½ cups.

Caesar Goes Wild Salad

This twist on the traditional Caesar salad uses oolichan instead of anchovies, as well as bannock croutons.

1 large egg
1 Smoked Oolichan fillet, poached (see note)
⅓ cup sunflower oil
1 clove garlic, minced
1 tsp lemon juice
¼ tsp dry mustard
¼ tsp white pepper
4 cups Romaine lettuce, washed and torn
1 cup Bannock Croutons (page 133)
¼ cup Parmesan cheese, grated

In a blender or food processor on high, combine egg, oolichan, oil, garlic, lemon juice, mustard, and pepper and blend until frothy and emulsified. Place lettuce in a salad bowl and toss in dressing. Top with croutons and cheese.

Makes 5 servings.

■ See page 65 on smoking oolichan, or smoked oolichan can be bought from specialty seafood markets or from online sources. To poach smoked oolichan, place in boiling water and continue to boil for 4 minutes, then strain.

Season's Harvest Salad with Cranberry Dressing

This simple salad is great served with any seafood dish.

2 cups Romaine lettuce, washed and torn
2 cup mixed wild greens
3 tbsp Cranberry Salad Dressing (below)

In a large salad bowl, combine lettuce, greens, and cranberry dressing and toss well.

Makes 2 servings.

CRANBERRY SALAD DRESSING

1 cup fresh cranberries
½ cup sweet dried cranberries
Whites of 2 large eggs
¼ cup Raspberry Vinegar (page 118)
1 tbsp ketchup
1 tsp white sugar
¼ cup onions, minced
¼ tsp garlic, minced
Pinch of celery salt
½ cup canola oil

In a blender or food processor on low, combine fresh and dried cranberries and chop until fine, then set aside in a bowl. In a blender or food processor on high, combine remaining ingredients and blend on high until emulsified. Add cranberries and blend until smooth. Store leftovers in a sealed container in the refrigerator.

Makes 1 cup.

Cucumber & Dill Salad

This refreshing salad is best served immediately while cucumbers are still crisp. A great accompaniment to Alder-Grilled Marinated Wild Salmon (page 59).

2 tbsp onions, chopped
2 cloves garlic, crushed
2 tsp pineapple juice
1 tsp teriyaki sauce
1 tsp corn syrup
1 tsp dried dill weed
½ tsp celery salt
½ tsp cayenne pepper
5 cups cucumbers, peeled, seeded, and cut into bite-sized pieces
1 cup French vanilla yogurt

In a blender or food processor on high, combine onions, garlic, pineapple juice, teriyaki sauce, syrup, dill weed, celery salt, and cayenne and blend until emulsified. In a large bowl, combine cucumbers, yogurt, and mixture, and toss well.

Makes 6 servings.

How To Cook Rice

WILD RICE

Wild rice is a long-grain aquatic grass seed. It has a nutty, earthy taste and is a good substitute for basmati rice. When fully cooked, the grain bursts open to reveal the white interior. Use with brown rice in the Wild Rice Medley (page 84).

1/3 **cup wild rice, uncooked**
1 **cup cold water**
Dash of salt

Soak and rinse wild rice in three changes of hot tap water to remove starch. In a saucepan on high heat, combine wild rice, water, and salt and bring to a boil. Reduce heat to low, cover with lid, and simmer for 20 minutes, then drain.

Makes 1 cup.

BROWN RICE

Brown rice is a long-grain seed that is a healthy accompaniment to any meal. It cooks to a chewy texture and has a nutty flavor. Use in the Wild Rice Medley (page 84).

1 **cup brown rice, uncooked**
2 **cups cold water**
1/4 **tsp salt**

Soak and rinse rice in three changes of hot tap water to remove starch. In saucepan on high heat, combine rice, water, and salt and bring to a boil. Reduce heat to low, cover with lid, and simmer for 20 minutes, then drain.

Makes 2 cups.

Wild Rice Medley

This dish is a healthy yet tasty combination of rice and vegetables. Serve with salmon, cod, and halibut dishes.

1 cup cooked wild rice (see page 83)
2 cups cooked brown rice (see page 83)
1 tbsp sunflower oil
1 tbsp onions, minced
1 tbsp carrots, minced
2 tsp celery, minced
2 tsp green bell peppers, minced
2 tsp red bell peppers, minced
¼ tsp garlic salt
¼ tsp ground cardamom

In a frying pan on medium, heat oil and sauté all ingredients, except rice, for 4 minutes, until softened. Add wild and brown rice to mixture and toss lightly.

Makes 4 servings.

■ For a great side dish, make a **Wild Rice Salad** by adding 3 tbsp of Mayonnaise (page 126) to 4 cups of chilled Wild Rice Medley.

Wild Rice Pancakes

For breakfast, serve Wild Rice Pancakes with maple syrup, or for a savory appetizer, with Raspberry Cranberry Chutney (page 117).

2 cups cooked wild rice (see page 83)
1 cup all-purpose flour
1 tsp baking powder
½ tsp salt
1 tsp white sugar
2 large eggs
¼ cup butter, melted
1 cup milk

In a bowl, combine rice, flour, baking powder, salt, and sugar and mix. Add remaining ingredients and mix well. Cover and refrigerate for 3 hours, allowing rice to absorb liquids. In an oiled skillet on medium heat, add 2 tsp of rice batter, then flatten out into an oval shape. Flip when edges turn brown. Repeat with rest of batter.

Makes 8 pancakes.

Pineapple-Arugula Wild Rice

This dish is great on its own, or when stuffed into Cornish game hens.

3 tbsp butter
1 tbsp onions, minced
2 tsp celery, minced
1 tbsp pineapple juice
1½ tbsp fresh arugula, coarsely chopped
5 cups cooked wild rice (see page 83)
¼ tsp freshly ground black pepper
¼ tsp dried dill weed
¼ tsp celery salt

In a frying pan on medium heat, melt butter. Stir in onions, celery, juice, and arugula. Reduce heat to low and sauté for 12 minutes until onions are translucent. Add rice, pepper, dill weed, and celery salt, and toss well.

Makes 6 servings.

Wild Rice Stuffing

A great treat for Thanksgiving or other occasions. This recipe makes enough to stuff a 10-pound turkey; Dolly also likes to use it to stuff pheasant.

²/₃ cup wild rice, uncooked
2 cups Chicken Stock (page 108)
¼ tsp salt
4 tbsp butter
2 cups celery, diced
3 cups onions, diced
½ cup mushrooms (optional)
3 cups Bannock Breadcrumbs (page 134)
¼ tsp celery salt
2 tsp black pepper
2 tsp fresh marjoram, minced
2 tsp fresh thyme, minced

Preheat oven to 350°F (180°C). Soak and rinse wild rice in three changes of hot tap water to remove starch. In a frying pan on high heat, bring rice, stock, and salt to a boil, then reduce heat to low. Cover with lid and simmer for 20 minutes, then strain. In a frying pan on medium heat, melt butter. Sauté celery, onions, and mushrooms for 3 minutes, until softened. In a baking dish, combine rice and vegetable mixtures with remaining ingredients and mix well. Cover with lid and bake for 45 minutes.

Makes 6 cups.

Wild Rice & Cheddar Cheese Casserole

This is a wonderful comfort food on a cold winter night.

1 cup cooked wild rice (see page 83)
2 tbsp onions, diced
1 tsp dried dill weed
¼ cup Crème Fraîche (page 127)
2 tbsp Cheddar cheese, shredded
1 tsp celery salt

Preheat oven to 350°F (180°C). In an oiled casserole dish, combine all ingredients and mix. Cover with lid and bake for 35 minutes.

Makes 2 servings.

Sweet Potato Tarts

Sweet potatoes originated in the Americas in countries such as Ecuador and Peru. Annie created this recipe when she wanted a faster, easier way to serve them. These tarts can also be served for dessert.

¼ cup sweet potatoes, peeled, quartered, boiled for 25 minutes, and mashed
¼ cup sweet condensed milk
1 tbsp brown sugar, lightly packed
2 tsp pastry flour
1½ tsp egg whites
2 tbsp whole milk
1 tsp butter, melted
Pinch of salt
Pinch of nutmeg
4 unbaked tart shells (3-in/7½-cm diameter each)
Ground hazelnuts (for garnish)

Preheat oven to 350°F (180°C). In a blender or food processor on high, combine cooked sweet potatoes, condensed milk, sugar, flour, and egg whites and blend until well mixed. Spoon into a large bowl and add whole milk, butter, salt, and nutmeg. Mix well, then pour filling into tart shells. Bake for 40 minutes, then let cool completely. Garnish with ground hazelnuts.

Makes 4 servings.

■ You can store these tarts in the refrigerator or freezer; to reheat, bake for 8 minutes in a preheated oven at 350°F (180°C).

Whipped Sweet Potatoes

A good substitute for mashed potatoes, this dish is great served alongside wild salmon.

3 cups sweet potatoes, peeled, quartered, boiled for 20 minutes, and mashed
¼ cup sweetened condensed milk, heated
¼ cup Crème Fraîche (page 127), heated
2 tbsp butter, softened
1 tsp Worcestershire sauce
½ tsp salt
¼ tsp black pepper
¼ tsp nutmeg

In a saucepan on medium heat, combine all ingredients, then sauté for 4 minutes and mix until texture is smooth.

Makes 4 servings.

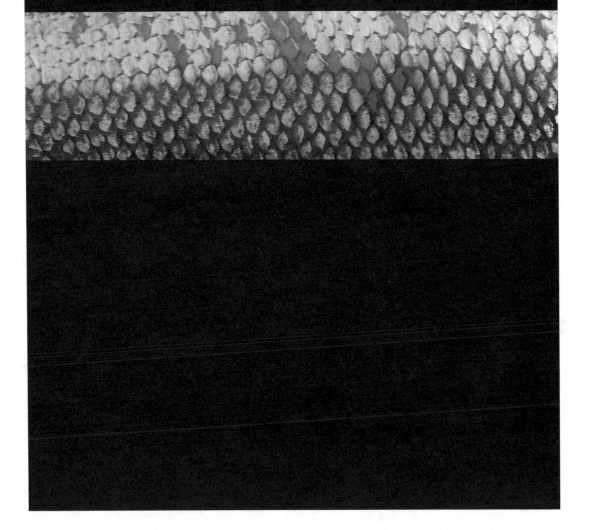

Soups & Stocks

Clearly Salmon Soup (Hagul Jam)

"Hagul jam" means "slow boil" in the Gitk'san language. Traditionally, as long ago as the pre-contact era, the Gitk'san would prepare this by pouring cold water into a cedar box or tightly woven basket, placing a heated rock inside, and then salmon.

½ cup onions, diced
2 cups potatoes, cut into bite-sized pieces
5 cups cold water
1 lb (450 g) salmon, cut into bite-sized pieces
Pinch of salt
Dried seaweed (for garnish)

In a large pot on high heat, bring onion, potatoes, and water to a boil. Continue to boil for 8 minutes. Add salmon and salt and remove from heat. Cover with lid and let stand 5 minutes (do not stir). Garnish each serving with seaweed.

Makes 5 servings.

Seaweed Salmon Roe Soup

We collected seaweed along the Pacific coast during the month of May, when the picking season lasts about three weeks. It was harvested at low tide and placed on rocks to dry for a few hours, then chopped and roasted for a crispy snack. Seaweed is an excellent vegetarian food as it contains protein from shellfish.

1½ cups Salmon Stock (page 106)
¼ cup dried seaweed, cut into bite-sized pieces
1 tbsp salmon roe (see note)
1 tbsp oolichan oil (optional) (see note)

In a large pot on high heat, bring stock to a boil. Add seaweed, roe, and oolichan oil. Remove immediately from heat and serve.

Makes 2 servings.

■ Salmon roe can be purchased at your local seafood or gourmet markets, or from online sources. You can also extract the roe yourself from a whole salmon (spring or chum is the best); remove the roe from the sac and boil until it turns orange in color and becomes spongy.

■ See page 166 for information on making oolichan oil, or oolichan oil may be bought from specialty seafood markets or from online sources. You may substitute oolichan oil with cod liver or seal oil.

Feast Venison Soup

A simple yet hearty soup that will warm and satisfy family and friends during winter.

3 tbsp sunflower oil
2 lbs (900 g) venison stew meat (see note)
4 cups Venison Stock (page 107)
4 cups potatoes, diced
Preserved vegetables from Venison Stock (page 107)

In a large pot on high, heat oil. Sear venison on all sides for 5 minutes until browned all over. Add stock and bring to a boil. Add potatoes and vegetables. Reduce heat to low and simmer for 12 minutes.

Makes 6 servings.

■ Venison stew meat can be purchased from gourmet butchers or from online sources.

Buffalo Cabbage Soup

Buffalo smokies are like the more familiar Bavarian smokies, except they are leaner and more mildly spiced.

½ cup green cabbage, shredded
½ cup purple cabbage, shredded
½ cup onions, diced
1 stalk celery, diced
2 buffalo smokies, sliced into bite-sized pieces (see note)
4 cups boiling water
1 tsp fresh cilantro leaves, chopped
Purple cabbage, shredded (for garnish)

In a large pot on high heat, combine all ingredients except garnish and bring to a boil. Continue to boil for 10 minutes. Reduce heat to low and simmer for 30 minutes. Garnish each serving with a few shreds of purple cabbage.

Makes 5 servings.

■ Buffalo smokies can be purchased from gourmet butchers or from online sources.

Venison & Wild Rice Soup

A creamy concoction of venison and wild rice; one of the most savory soups you will come across.

1 lb (450 g) ground lean venison (see note)
1 tbsp canola oil
1 cup cooked wild rice (see page 83)
1 can Cream of Potato Soup (10 oz/300 ml)
1 tsp garlic powder
1 cup whole milk
½ cup Cheddar cheese, shredded
Fresh parsley (for garnish)

In a large pot on high, heat oil and sauté venison until browned all over. Drain fat from pot and set aside. In a bowl, combine cooked rice and remaining ingredients except parsley and mix well. Add to venison and return pot to medium heat and simmer until cheese is melted. Garnish each serving with parsley.

Makes 6 servings.

■ Ground venison can be purchased from gourmet butchers or from online sources.

Shiitake Mushroom & Wild Rice Soup

This is a tasty and nourishing soup for a cold winter's night.

3 cups Chicken Stock (page 108)
½ cup leeks, thinly sliced
1½ cups cooked wild rice (see page 83)
1 cup whole shiitake mushrooms, chopped into bite-sized pieces
Preserved vegetables from Chicken Stock (page 108)
¼ cup white wine (Chardonnay is good)
1¾ cups Crème Fraîche (page 127), heated
2 tbsp butter
¼ tsp salt
¼ tsp black pepper
¼ tsp dried cilantro leaves (coriander)

In a large pot on high heat, bring stock and leeks to a boil, then reduce heat to low.
Add rice, cover with lid, and simmer for 50 minutes. Stir in all remaining ingredients,
cover with lid, and simmer for an additional 10 minutes.

Makes 6 servings.

Crab & Corn Soup

A creamy and nutritious soup that tastes best with fresh crab.

2 cups Salmon Stock (page 106)
2 slices bacon, fried and diced, reserve 2 tbsp bacon fat
1½ cups whole milk
1 cup Crème Fraîche (page 127)
2 tbsp cornstarch
1 cup corn kernels
½ cup fresh cooked crabmeat, diced
½ tsp salt
¼ tsp white pepper
Bacon bits (for garnish)

In a large pot on high heat, bring stock to a boil, then add bacon and bacon fat. In another large pot on medium, combine milk, crème fraîche, and cornstarch (stirring to prevent clumps), and cook for 6 minutes. Then add stock mixture, simmer for an additional 6 minutes or until it thickens. Add corn, crab, salt, and pepper and continue to simmer for an additional 8 minutes. Garnish each serving with bacon bits.

Makes 4 servings.

Hominy Corn Soup

Hominy is dried corn kernels that have been treated with an alkali to remove the hulls, making it easier to digest.

2 lbs (900 g) pork hocks
7 cups boiling water
½ cup celery, minced
1 cup carrots, minced
¼ cup onions, diced
2 cups canned whole white hominy corn kernels, drained (see note)
1 cup kidney beans, cooked
¼ tsp horseradish sauce
1 clove garlic, minced
Pinch of salt
Pinch of white pepper

In a large pot on medium heat, simmer pork hocks in water for 2 hours. Remove from heat and let cool. Remove pork hocks to cut away any meat into bite-sized pieces and return to the soup, then discard the hocks. Skim off fat and discard. Return pot on high heat, add remaining ingredients, and bring to a boil. Reduce heat to medium and simmer for 8 minutes until vegetables are tender.

Makes 6 servings.

■ Canned whole white hominy corn kernels are available in most grocery stores. If using dried hominy, soak overnight before cooking.

Butternut Squash Soup

An essential soup for autumn that is easy to make.

2½ cups Vegetable Stock (page 109)
Preserved butternut squash and vegetables from Vegetable Stock (see page 109)
2 tbsp maple syrup
½ tsp allspice
¼ cup Crème Fraîche (page 127), heated
Sour cream (for garnish)

In a large pot on high heat, combine all ingredients, except crème fraîche and garnish, and bring to a boil. Reduce heat to low and simmer for 5 minutes. Remove from heat and let cool completely. In a blender or food processor on high, add crème fraîche and soup and pulse until blended. Garnish each serving with a dollop of sour cream.

Makes 4 servings.

Tomato Potato Soup

This vegetarian soup makes a perfect light lunch.

1 tbsp sunflower oil
½ cup green bell pepper, diced
½ cup onions, diced
½ stalk celery, diced
2 cloves garlic, minced
2 tbsp fresh basil, minced
¼ tsp dried marjoram
¼ tsp jalapeño peppers, stemmed, seeded, and minced
¼ tsp black pepper
1 can tomatoes (10 oz/300 ml), diced (reserve the juice)
2 cups Vegetable Stock (page 109)
2 cups potatoes, diced

In large pot on high, heat oil. Add peppers, onions, celery, and garlic and sauté, stirring continually until onions are softened. Add basil, marjoram, jalapeños, and pepper and mix well. Continue to sauté for 5 minutes, stirring frequently. Add only the juice of the can of the tomatoes and vegetable stock. Lower heat to medium and simmer for 10 minutes. Add tomatoes and potatoes and continue to simmer for 1½ hours.

Makes 4 servings.

Smoked Salmon Chowder

This hearty chowder can be served as an entrée. Serve with a side of bannock.

2 tbsp canola oil
2 cups potatoes, diced
2 tbsp all-purpose flour
4 cups Salmon Stock (page 106)
1 cup smoked salmon, coarsely chopped
Preserved vegetables from Salmon Stock (page 106)
1 tsp fresh parsley, minced
¼ tsp salt
¼ tsp black pepper
1 tsp fresh thyme, minced
Pinch of dried dill weed
Dried seaweed (for garnish)
Sour cream (for garnish)

In a large pot on high, heat oil. Add potatoes and sauté for 6 minutes. Reduce heat to medium, stir in flour and stock and bring to a boil, stirring constantly. Add salmon, vegetables, salt, pepper, parsley, thyme, and dill weed. Cook for 3 minutes, stirring continually. Garnish each serving with a sprinkle of seaweed and a dollop of sour cream.

Makes 4 servings.

Clam Chowder

This recipe brings back memories of clam digging with relatives at Nanoose Bay on Vancouver Island.

1½ slices bacon, diced
¼ cup onions
4 potatoes, chopped into bite-sized pieces
½ cup carrots, diced
½ cup celery, diced
4 cups boiling water
2 cans whole baby clams (5 oz/150 ml each) (reserve nectar)
1 tsp salt
¼ tsp black pepper

In a large pot on high heat, sauté bacon, onions, potatoes, carrots, and celery for 7 minutes. Add water, clams, reserved nectar, salt, and pepper. Bring to a boil, then reduce heat to medium and simmer for 3 minutes.

Makes 6 servings.

Buffalo Hominy Corn Chowder

This is a very hearty chowder. Serve with Just Like Grandma's Bannock (page 130).

1½ cups dried hominy (see note)
1 tsp canola oil
4 buffalo smokies, chopped into bite-sized pieces (see note)
½ cup celery, diced
4 green onions, minced
2 tbsp butter
2 tbsp all-purpose flour
2 tbsp mustard
1 tsp Worcestershire sauce
½ tsp dried marjoram
2 cups cold water
1½ cups whole milk
1 cup Crème Fraîche (page 127)
½ cup mushrooms, sliced
¼ tsp salt
¼ tsp black pepper

The night before preparing chowder, soak hominy in 3 cups cold water and let sit overnight. The next day, in a frying pan on high, heat oil. Add buffalo smokies, celery, and onions and sauté for 4 minutes until onions are soft, then set aside. In a large pot on medium heat, melt butter and add flour, mustard, Worcestershire sauce, and marjoram and stir until thick and bubbly. Add water, milk, crème fraîche, drained hominy, mushrooms, salt, pepper, and smokies, celery, and onion mixture. Simmer for 30 minutes, stirring continually.

Makes 4 servings.

■ Hominy is available in the dried foods section of most grocery stores.

■ Buffalo smokies can be purchased at local gourmet butchers or specialty markets or from online sources.

Salmon Head Broth

No part of a fish goes to waste in First Nations cuisine; even a salmon's nose, eyes, and cheeks are consumed. Broth from the boiled head is served hot in a cup with bannock on the side. The broth has a rich and buttery taste, and if you're brave, you can eat the head too!

2 large salmon heads, blood and gills scraped away
½ tsp salt
Boiling water (to cover)

Split each head in half and sprinkle with salt. In a saucepan on medium heat, boil heads for 30 minutes in just enough boiling water to cover them. Remove heads. If not using immediately, cool broth quickly in an ice bath, stirring continually to prevent bacterial growth, and store in the freezer.

Makes 2 servings.

Salmon Stock

This stock is used in the Crab Mousse (page 46), Seaweed Salmon Roe Soup (page 93), Smoked Salmon Chowder (page 102), and Crab & Corn Soup (page 98).

Fish bones from 1 large (10 lbs/4½ kg) salmon (see note)
5 cups boiling water
½ cup onions, diced
½ cup carrots, diced
½ cup celery, diced
2 tbsp butter
¼ tsp salt
Pinch of white pepper
¼ tsp dried thyme

Rinse fish bones under cold running water for 5 minutes. In a stockpot on high heat, combine all ingredients and bring to a boil. Reduce heat to low and simmer for 1 hour, then strain stock into a container. If not using immediately, cool stock quickly in an ice bath, stirring continually to prevent bacterial growth, and store in the freezer.

Makes 4 cups.

■ You can debone the salmon yourself, or get fish bones from your fishmonger.

Venison Stock

Venison stock is a great alternative for any recipe that calls for beef stock. Use both the stock and the vegetables in the Venison Stew (page 22) and Feast Venison Soup (page 94), or just the stock in the Venison & Wild Rice Casserole (page 24).

1 lb (450 g) venison bones (see note)
6 cups boiling water
2 cups onions, diced
1 cup celery, diced
¼ tsp marjoram
¼ tsp salt
¼ tsp black pepper

Preheat oven to 500°F (260°C). Place bones on a baking sheet and roast for 1 hour, until golden brown. In a stockpot on high heat, bring roasted bones and remaining ingredients to a boil, then reduce heat to low and simmer for 2 hours, skimming off and discarding foam from the surface. Strain. If not using immediately, cool stock quickly in an ice bath, stirring continually to prevent bacterial growth, and store in the freezer.

Makes 4 cups.

■ Venison bones can be ordered from your local gourmet butcher or from online sources.

Chicken Stock

Use both the stock and the vegetables in the Duck & Wild Rice Casserole (page 36), or the stock on its own in the Wild Rice Stuffing (page 87) and Shiitake Mushroom & Wild Rice Soup (page 97).

1 lb (450 g) chicken bones
2 cups onions, chopped
1 cup celery, chopped
1 cup carrots, chopped
Pinch of salt
½ tsp garlic, chopped
½ tsp poultry seasoning
6 cups boiling water

In a stockpot on high heat, bring all ingredients to a boil. Reduce heat to low and simmer for 2 hours, skimming off and discarding foam from the surface. Strain. If not using immediately, cool stock quickly in an ice bath, stirring continually to prevent bacterial growth, and store in the freezer.

Makes 4 cups.

Vegetable Stock

Use both the stock and the vegetables in the Butternut Squash Soup (page 100), or stock on its own in the Bounty of the Sea (page 54) and the Basil & Garlic Tomato Sauce (page 122).

2 tbsp canola oil
¼ cup onions, chopped
¼ cup celery, chopped
¾ cup carrots, chopped
¼ cup sweet potatoes, chopped
¼ cup Russet potatoes, chopped
1½ cups butternut squash, chopped
½ cup mushrooms, chopped
½ tsp garlic, minced
3 tbsp fresh thyme, chopped
1½ tsp celery salt
¼ tsp allspice
7 cups cold water

In a stockpot on high, heat oil. Add onions and celery and sauté until onions are softened. Add remaining ingredients and bring to a boil. Reduce heat to low and simmer 1½ hours, skimming off and discarding foam from surface. Strain and use immediately or let cool, then store in freezer.

Makes 2½ cups.

Sauces & Condiments

Wild Smoked Salmon Cream Cheese

Serve this spread with Just Like Grandma's Bannock (page 130), Spicy Cornsticks (page 136), or Bannock Cheesesticks (page 132).

3 oz (85 g) Half-Smoked Whole Salmon (see notes)
¼ cup boiling water
2 cups cream cheese

In a microwave-safe bowl, place salmon in water and heat on high in microwave for 3 minutes to poach. Drain and remove any skin from salmon. In a blender or food processor, combine salmon and cream cheese and blend until smooth. Store leftovers in a sealed container in the refrigerator.

Makes 2 cups.

- Please be sure not to use fully smoked salmon in this recipe as half-smoked salmon is more moist.

- See page 165 for information on making Half-Smoked Whole Salmon, or if you prefer, purchase half-smoked salmon in the seafood section at markets or wherever smoked salmon is sold.

Alder-Grilled Butternut Squash (page 70), Zucchini & Corn Medley (page 71), and Blackberry-Glazed Beets (page 73)

Roasted Yam & Feta Salad (page 77)

Wild Rice Pancakes (page 85) with Raspberry Cranberry Chutney (page 117)

Just Like Grandma's Bannock (page 130)

Tangy Rhubarb Sauce

Rhubarb is a unique vegetable that is often overlooked in cooking. Dolly's family always had a lot of rhubarb (called "qatl'okwaots" in Gitk'san) growing in the garden alongside the strawberries. Rhubarb is picked before the first week in July, otherwise it gets bitter and tough. Tangy Rhubarb Sauce is a great dipping sauce for the Wild Buffalo Smokies (page 26) or any wild game dish.

½ tsp sunflower oil
1 cup rhubarb, diced
½ cup onions, diced
1 in (2½ cm) fresh ginger, peeled and grated
½ cup apple cider vinegar
¼ tsp salt
1 cup brown sugar
1 cup Raspberry Syrup (page 176)
¼ tsp cayenne pepper
½ tsp allspice
1 tsp dried rosemary

In a saucepan on high, heat oil. Sauté rhubarb, onions, and ginger for 10 minutes until rhubarb is softened. Add remaining ingredients, reduce heat to medium, and simmer for 30 minutes, stirring frequently. Store leftovers in a sealed container in the refrigerator.

Makes 1½ cups.

Honey Dijon Dip

Serve with Oven-Roasted Rabbit (page 30) or as a dressing for mixed green salad.

1½ tsp Dijon mustard
1 tsp honey
1 tbsp sunflower oil
1 tbsp apple cider vinegar
Pinch of ground cardamom

In a blender or food processor on high, combine all ingredients and blend until emulsified. Store leftovers in a sealed container in the refrigerator.

Makes ½ cup.

Blackberry Vinegar

Blackberries are a great summertime treat. Use this vinegar in the Blackberry-Glazed Beets (page 73) and the Black Poppy Seed Dressing (page 79).

1 cup blackberries
1 cup white vinegar
1 cup water
2 cups caster (superfine) sugar

In a bowl, combine blackberries, vinegar, and water and let sit for 12 hours. Strain mixture through a sieve or jelly bag. In a saucepan on high heat, combine strained blackberry liquid and sugar and bring to a boil. Continue to boil for 10 minutes, then pour into a sterilized Mason jar. Tighten lid and let cool. Store in a dry, cool place.

Makes 2½ cups.

- **Blackberry Balsamic Vinegar:** To make blackberry balsamic vinegar, use balsamic vinegar instead of white vinegar, triple the quantities of ingredients, and after adding sugar, let it reduce on low heat or in a crockpot for 16 hours.

Raspberry Zinger Sauce

Brush this tangy sauce on meats during the last few minutes of barbecuing, or use with the Oven-Baked Venison Skewers (page 19) or Fast Fish Hash (page 61).

1 tsp sunflower oil
1 tbsp butter
½ cup onions, diced
½ tsp pineapple juice
5 tbsp Raspberry Balsamic Vinegar (page 118)
2 cups ketchup
1 tsp dry mustard
½ cup white sugar
½ tsp soy sauce
½ tsp white pepper
¼ tsp ginger, powdered
1 clove garlic, minced
½ tsp cayenne pepper

In a saucepan on high, heat oil and butter. Sauté onions for 6 minutes until softened. Reduce heat to low, add all remaining ingredients, and simmer for 30 minutes, stirring occasionally. Let cool, then store in a sealed container in refrigerator.

Makes 2 cups.

Raspberry Cranberry Chutney

A zesty chutney perfect with Wild Shepherd's Pie (page 20) or the Wild Rice Pancakes (page 85).

1 tsp sunflower oil
½ cup onions, diced
1½ cups Raspberry Syrup (page 176)
½ cup raspberries
1 cup cranberries
½ cup sweetened dried cranberries
2 cups Raspberry Vinegar (page 118)
½ tsp orange zest
½ tsp fresh ginger zest
¼ tsp allspice
¼ tsp nutmeg
¼ tsp dried cilantro (coriander)

In a saucepan on high, heat oil. Sauté onions for 6 minutes until softened. Add syrup and bring to a boil. Add remaining ingredients and boil for an additional 2 minutes. Reduce heat to low and simmer for 15 minutes, stirring occasionally. Remove from heat and let cool. Store in a sealed container in the refrigerator.

Makes 3 cups.

Raspberry Vinegar

Use this vinegar in recipes such as Sweet & Tangy Purple Cabbage (page 74), Roasted New Potato Salad (page 78), and Cranberry Salad Dressing (page 81).

1 cup raspberries
1 cup white vinegar
1 cup water
2 cups caster (superfine) sugar

In a bowl, combine raspberries, vinegar, and water and let sit for 12 hours. Strain mixture through a sieve or jelly bag. In a saucepan on high heat, combine strained raspberry liquid and sugar and bring to a boil. Continue to boil for 10 minutes, then pour into a sterilized Mason jar. Tighten lid and let cool. Store in a dry, cool place.

Makes 2½ cups.

- **Raspberry Balsamic Vinegar:** To make raspberry balsamic vinegar, use balsamic vinegar instead of white vinegar, triple the quantities of ingredients, and after adding sugar, let it reduce on low heat or in a crockpot for 16 hours.

Juniper Berry Sauce

Whole juniper berries are slightly soft, purple fruit with a pine flavor. Serve with wild game dishes.

¼ cup sour cream
¼ cup Mayonnaise (page 126)
½ tsp dried juniper berries, finely ground (see note)

In a bowl, whisk together sour cream and mayonnaise, then blend in berries. Store in a sealed container in the refrigerator.

Makes ½ cup.

■ Dried juniper berries can be found in the herb and spice section in grocery stores.

Spicy Corn Salsa

Fire up your tastebuds with this fresh salsa. Serve with Grandma's Spicy Crab Cakes (page 45).

1 cup corn kernels
3 cups tomatoes, chopped
¼ cup onions, minced
1 clove garlic, minced
2 tsp jalapeño peppers, stemmed, seeded, and minced (see note)
1 tsp horseradish sauce
¼ cup Raspberry Balsamic Vinegar (page 118)
¼ cup corn oil
½ tsp cornstarch
2 tbsp fresh parsley, minced
½ tsp celery salt
¼ tsp black pepper
½ tsp cayenne pepper

In a saucepan on high, combine all ingredients and bring to a boil. Reduce heat to low and simmer for 10 minutes.

Makes 3 cups.

■ Wash your hands thoroughly after handling jalapeño peppers.

Hominy Corn Relish

Hominy is dried corn kernels that have been treated with an alkali (e.g., lye- or lime-water) to remove the hulls, making the corn easier to digest. It can be purchased in the dried foods section at the market or specialty stores.

2 cups canned hominy corn kernels (see note)
1/3 cup white sugar
1 tsp cornstarch
1/2 cup white vinegar
1/4 cup onions, diced
1/2 cup celery, diced
1 tsp celery salt
1 tbsp prepared mustard
Dash of white pepper
Dash of Tabasco sauce
1/2 cup cooked black beans
1/2 cup cooked red kidney beans

In a saucepan on high heat, combine all ingredients except beans and whisk together. Bring to a boil, then continue to boil for 5 minutes. Remove from heat and cool. Add beans and mix well. Store in a sealed container in the refrigerator.

Makes 3 1/2 cups.

■ Canned hominy corn kernels are available at most grocery stores. If using dried hominy, soak overnight then drain before cooking.

Basil & Garlic Tomato Sauce

This tasty sauce is excellent with seafood dishes such as Bounty of the Sea (page 54).

4 tsp sunflower oil
2 tbsp butter
1 cup onions, minced
½ cup carrots, minced
½ cup celery, minced
2 cloves garlic, minced
2 cups Vegetable Stock (page 109)
3 cups tomatoes, seeded and minced
4 tsp tomato paste
¼ tsp white sugar
4 tsp fresh basil, minced
1 tsp dried thyme
Pinch of celery salt
1 tsp cayenne pepper

In a saucepan on medium, heat oil and butter. Sauté onions, carrots, celery, and garlic for 20 minutes until softened. Add remaining ingredients and cook for an additional 30 minutes, until sauce thickens. Remove from heat and let cool before using. Store leftovers in a sealed container in the refrigerator.

Makes 4 cups.

Brown Mushroom Gravy

Drizzle this earthy gravy on the Alder-Grilled Marinated Elk (page 16) or Alder-Grilled Marinated Venison Chops (page 17).

2 tbsp butter
2 tsp cornstarch
¾ cup mushrooms, finely sliced
½ tsp garlic salt
¼ tsp celery salt
10 green peppercorns
¼ tsp dried marjoram
¼ tsp dried cilantro (coriander)
2½ cups Beef Stock (below)

In a saucepan on high heat, melt butter. Stir in cornstarch, mushrooms, garlic salt, celery salt, peppercorns, marjoram, and cilantro and reduce heat to medium, stirring continually for 5 minutes. Reduce heat to low and add stock. Simmer for 20 minutes until it thickens.

Makes 1¾ cups.

BEEF STOCK

10 oz (275 g) beef bones
3¾ cups boiling water
1¼ cups onions, diced
⅝ cup celery, diced
⅝ cup carrots, diced
¼ tsp garlic, minced
Dash of dried marjoram
Dash of dried thyme

In a stockpot on high heat, bring all ingredients to a boil. Reduce heat to low and simmer for 2 hours, skimming off and discarding foam. Strain before using.

Makes 2½ cups.

Sweet & Tangy Sauce

Serve warm with Venison Meatballs (page 18) or Clam Fritters (page 50).

2 tbsp carrots, minced
2 tbsp celery, minced
½ tsp ginger zest
½ tsp garlic, minced
½ cup brown sugar
1 tbsp cornstarch
½ tsp ketchup
⅓ cup Raspberry Vinegar (page 118)
2 tbsp soy sauce
¼ cup pineapple juice
2 tsp cold water

In a blender or food processor on high, combine all ingredients until emulsified. In a saucepan on high heat, add mixture and whisk continually for 10 minutes until it boils and thickens. Store in a sealed container in the refrigerator.

Makes 1 cup.

Dill Sauce

A classic recipe best served with salmon, halibut, or cod dishes.

¼ cup sour cream
¼ cup Mayonnaise (page 126)
¼ tsp dried dill weed

In a bowl, whisk all ingredients together until smooth. Serve immediately or store in a sealed container in the refrigerator.

Makes ½ cup.

Mayonnaise

A not-too-difficult alternative to store-bought mayonnaise. Use high-quality, farm-fresh eggs where possible, since the yolks are not cooked.

Yolks of 2 large eggs
1½ cups sunflower oil
1 tsp prepared mustard
2 tsp apple cider vinegar
2 tsp lemon juice
½ tsp white sugar
1 tsp salt
1 tsp white pepper

In a bowl, whisk egg yolks continually for 2 minutes. Continue whisking and add oil, 1 tbsp at a time. Add remaining ingredients and whisk until mixture becomes thick and creamy. Store in a sealed container in the refrigerator.

Makes 1 cup.

Crème Fraîche

This is a great substitute for any heavy cream that has to be heated, as regular heavy cream curdles easily.

2 cups whipping cream, pasteurized
½ cup cultured buttermilk (see note)

In a saucepan on high heat, bring whipping cream to a boil. Remove from heat immediately and add buttermilk. Leave covered with plastic wrap on the counter for 12 hours, until thick. If desired, let sit an additional 12 hours for a fuller flavor.

Makes 2 cups.

■ Cultured buttermilk is a low-fat skim milk, the most common form of buttermilk sold in supermarkets. It contains a healthy bacteria culture similar to yogurt. Store in a sealed container in the refrigerator for up to 1 week.

Savory Red Currant Jelly

Use with the Venison Roast with Juniper Berry Rub (page 21).

1 tbsp sunflower oil
1 cup onions, minced
1 clove garlic, minced
2½ cups red currants
2½ cups caster (superfine) sugar, warmed
4 tsp fresh rosemary, chopped

In a saucepan on high, heat oil and sauté onions and garlic for 10 minutes. Reduce heat to low, add currants and sugar, and cook for 10 minutes, continually crushing the berries as they soften. Increase the heat to high and boil rapidly for 10 minutes, stirring continually. Pour through a sieve into a container. Store leftovers in a sealed container in the refrigerator.

Makes 3½ cups.

Baked Goods & Desserts

Just Like Grandma's Bannock

Bannock ("ajam anaek" in Gitk'san) is a traditional pan-fried bread adopted into the Native North American cuisine in the eighteenth century from the Scottish fur traders' "griddle scones." Dolly's first business was selling bannock from a food cart outside the Museum of Anthropology at the University of British Columbia; her Native customers often told her, "It tastes just like Grandma's bannock!" hence the name. Bannock is delicious and can be served with preserves or Apple-Pear Butter (page 178) as a special treat. It also makes a great sandwich bun by cutting the bannock in half; try stuffing it with Wild Smoked Salmon Cream Cheese (page 112) or Venison Pâté (page 23).

7 cups all-purpose flour
1½ cups lukewarm water (105°F/41°C)
   (see note)
1½ tsp salt

2¼ tsp white sugar
1 tbsp canola oil
¾ tsp instant yeast
Canola oil (for frying)

In a large bowl, add flour and make a hole in the center. In a separate bowl, combine water, salt, sugar, 1 tbsp canola oil, and yeast, and stir. Pour into the hole in the flour and mix together by hand to form dough. Turn dough onto a lightly floured surface and knead for 10 minutes. Place dough in a sealed container or covered bowl and let rise at room temperature for 2 hours. On a lightly floured surface, roll out dough to a ½-in (1-cm) thickness, then cut into 2½-in (6½-cm) squares (see note). In a large frying pan on high, heat 2 in (5 cm) of oil. As soon as the square of dough is dropped into the hot oil, turn it 3 times so that it puffs up evenly. Repeat with several pieces at a time and fry until golden brown for 3 minutes on each side until all the dough has been fried.

Makes 25 small bannock.

- Make sure to use lukewarm water; if it is too hot or too cold, the yeast won't properly activate.

- For large bannock, cut into 4-in (10-cm) squares. For medium bannock, cut in 3-in (8-cm) squares.

- **Cinnamon & Brown Sugar Bannock:** For a coffee break or midday treat, lightly spread softened butter over freshly made bannock and sprinkle with a mixture of cinnamon and brown sugar.

Baked Bannock (Es'Pow'Dis)

Once bannock was incorporated into the Gitk'san cuisine, it also was prepared "Indian-style" in an earth oven, using tin containers that protected the dough yet still allowed it to rise. This baked bannock is delicious served either warm or at room temperature.

2 cups whole wheat flour
3 cups all-purpose flour
2½ tbsp baking powder
3 tbsp white sugar
1½ tsp salt
½ cup all-vegetable shortening
1 cup half-and-half cream
1½ cups cold water

Preheat oven to 375°F (190°C). In a large bowl, combine all ingredients and mix well (texture should be sticky). Pour into a 13x9x2-in (33x23x5-cm) pan and let sit for 5 minutes. Bake for 45 minutes until golden brown and dough shrinks away from the sides of the pan. Remove from oven and wrap in a clean, dry cloth until ready to serve.

Makes 10 servings.

Savory Bannock Cheesesticks

Hunters and fishermen have been known to make bannock, or "bread-on-a-stick," over a campfire. Try substituting your favorite cheeses in this recipe.

Just Like Grandma's Bannock (page 130), unbaked dough
¾ cup Parmesan cheese, freshly grated
¾ cup Gruyère cheese, freshly grated
½ cup Cheddar cheese, freshly grated
2 tsp garlic salt
2 large eggs

Preheat oven to 300°F (150°C). Prepare bannock dough and let rise for 2 hours. In a bowl, combine cheeses and garlic salt and mix, then set aside. In another bowl, slightly beat eggs and set aside. On a lightly floured surface, roll dough out by hand into 25 sticks (4x1 in/1x2½ cm each). Dip each stick into eggs, then into cheese mixture, and place on greased baking sheets with enough space between them so they will rise properly. Bake for 40 minutes.

Makes 25 cheesesticks.

Bannock Croutons

These crunchy croutons can be used to top the Caesar Goes Wild Salad (page 80) or any mixed greens.

2 prepared Just Like Grandma's Bannock (page 130), cut into bite-sized pieces
2 tsp butter, softened
¼ tsp garlic salt

Preheat oven to 300°F (150°C). In a bowl, combine bannock pieces and butter and mix. Sprinkle with garlic salt. Place on an ungreased baking sheet and bake for 10 minutes until crisp.

Makes 2 cups.

Bannock Breadcrumbs

Use these breadcrumbs in the Pacific Macaroni & Cheese (page 48), Venison Meatballs (page 18), Wild Rice Stuffing (page 87), and Grandma's Spicy Crabcakes (page 45). The breadcrumbs store well in the freezer.

4 large, prepared Just Like Grandma's Bannock (page 130), cut into bite-sized pieces

Preheat oven to 300°F (150°C). Place bannock pieces in a single layer onto a lightly greased baking sheet and bake for 9 minutes, turning at least once. (Do not overbake as they will become too hard.) Let cool for 5 minutes. In a blender or food processor on high, process bread until it becomes fine crumbs.

Makes 3 cups.

Bannock Crackers

These bite-sized morsels can be used for the Pemmican Canapés (page 28).

1 large Just Like Grandma's Bannock, unbaked dough (page 130)
Canola oil (for deep frying)

Preheat oven to 500°F (260°C). On a lightly floured surface, roll dough into a 4-in (10-cm) cylinder shape. In a large frying pan on high, heat 2 in (5 cm) of oil. As soon as the dough is dropped into the hot oil, turn it 3 times so that it puffs up evenly. Fry for 8 minutes, until golden brown. Remove from pan and let cool, then slice into 8 round crackers (½-in/1-cm thick) and place on a baking sheet. Toast for 3 minutes on both sides until golden brown.

Makes 8 crackers.

Spicy Cornsticks

Guests will enjoy these on their own or with softened butter. Prepare them using a cornstick pan (which has cornstick molds in it).

1 cup all-purpose flour
½ cup yellow cornmeal
1 cup corn kernels
4 tsp jalapeño peppers, stemmed, seeded, and minced (see note)
1 large egg
2 tsp baking powder
1 tsp baking soda
¼ cup corn oil
1 tbsp white sugar
½ tsp salt
½ cup whipping cream
¾ cup cold water

Preheat oven to 350°F (180°C). In a large bowl, combine all ingredients and mix well until dough resembles a thick paste. Spread evenly into a lightly greased cornstick pan and bake for 25 minutes. Remove from oven and let cool before serving.

Makes 18 cornsticks.

■ Wash your hands thoroughly after handling jalapeño peppers.

Wild Blueberry Cobbler

The wild berries in this recipe have a sweet, slightly tart flavor. Serve warm with vanilla ice cream and caramel sauce.

¾ cup buttermilk
1 large egg, beaten
2¼ cups all-purpose flour
3 tbsp white sugar
1 tbsp baking powder
½ tsp baking soda
½ tsp salt
¼ cup butter
¾ cup white sugar
½ tsp ground nutmeg
½ tsp cinnamon
2 envelopes unflavored gelatin (¼ oz/7 g each)
¼ cup boiling water
5 cups wild blueberries

Preheat oven to 375°F (190°C). In a bowl, combine buttermilk, egg, flour, 3 tbsp sugar, baking powder, baking soda, and salt, and mix well. Cut in butter and set aside. In another bowl, combine ¾ cup sugar, nutmeg, cinnamon, and gelatin, and mix, then set aside. In a saucepan on high heat, combine water and 2½ cups of the blueberries and bring to a boil. Add gelatin mixture, then reduce heat to low and simmer for 7 minutes, stirring continually. Remove from heat, then add remainder of berries. Spread mixture into an 8x8x2-in (20x20x5-cm) baking dish. Spoon dough evenly on top of berries. Bake for 25 minutes uncovered, or until golden brown, then cover with a lid or tinfoil and bake for an additional 10 minutes. Remove from oven and let cool completely, then refrigerate for 3 hours to allow berries to set.

Makes 10 servings.

Wild Berry Crisp

After enjoying a seafood or wild game dish, top off the evening with this Wild Berry Crisp. Serve when berries are in season, with Caramel Pecan Sauce (page 147) and whipped cream or vanilla ice cream.

1 cup boiling water
5 cups blueberries
2 cups strawberries, sliced
2 cups blackberries
2 envelopes unflavored gelatin (¼ oz/7 g each)
1¼ cups white sugar
2 cups pastry flour
2 cups rolled oat flakes
1 tsp baking powder
1 cup brown sugar
1 tsp salt
½ tsp nutmeg
1 cup margarine, chilled

Preheat oven to 375°F (190°C). In a saucepan on high heat, combine water, 2½ cups blueberries, 1 cup strawberries, and 1 cup blackberries and bring to a boil. In a bowl, combine gelatin and white sugar and mix, then add to hot berry mixture. Reduce heat to low and simmer for 10 minutes, stirring continually. Remove from heat, then add remaining berries. Spread berry mixture into a 13x9x2-in (33x23x5-cm) baking dish. In the bowl of an electric mixer, combine flour, oat flakes, baking powder, brown sugar, salt, nutmeg, and margarine and mix. Spread over berry mixture. Bake for 25 minutes, uncovered, then cover with a lid or tinfoil and bake for an additional 10 minutes. Let cool completely then refrigerate for 3 hours, allowing berries to set. Heat before serving.

Makes 10 servings.

Wild Berry Bannock Bread Pudding

Dolly tried using bannock in bread pudding instead of white bread and found that it had more flavor. Serve warm with vanilla ice cream and Caramel Pecan Sauce (page 147).

3½ cups whole milk, warmed
¼ cup white sugar
Drop of vanilla extract
1 tsp ground nutmeg
2 large eggs
5 cups prepared Just Like Grandma's Bannock (page 130), cut into bite-sized
      pieces
Whites of 4 large eggs
1 tsp cream of tartar
½ cup boiling water
1 cup blackberries
2 cups blueberries
1 cup strawberries, sliced
1 cup raspberries
1 cup white sugar

Preheat oven to 350°F (180°C). In a bowl, combine milk, ¼ cup sugar, vanilla, and nutmeg and mix well, then set aside. In another bowl, beat 2 large eggs, then add to milk mixture. Add bannock and allow it to soak for 30 minutes. In a stainless steel bowl, whip egg whites and cream of tartar to stiff peaks. Fold into bread mixture, then set aside. In a saucepan on high heat, combine water, ½ cup blackberries, 1 cup blueberries, ½ cup strawberries, and ½ cup raspberries and bring to a boil. Add 1 cup sugar, then reduce heat to low and simmer until thick. Remove from heat, then add remaining berries. In a 13x9x2-in (33x22x5-cm) baking pan, spread a thin layer of bread mixture, then top with a layer of berries. Repeat layers until mixtures are used up, ending with berries on top. Bake uncovered for 25 minutes until golden brown.

Makes 10 servings.

Blackberry Pie

Serve this pie with ice cream or whipped cream and Caramel Pecan Sauce (page 147).

¾ cup white sugar
1 envelope unflavored gelatin (¼ oz/7 g)
½ tsp allspice
3 cups blackberries
1 tbsp butter
¼ cup blackberry juice
Basic Pastry Dough, prepared (page 38)

Preheat oven to 350°F (180°C). In a bowl, combine sugar, gelatin, and allspice and mix well, then set aside. In a saucepan on high heat, combine 1½ cups blackberries, butter, juice, and sugar mixture and bring to a boil. Remove from heat and stir in remaining berries. On a lightly floured surface, roll out pastry dough into 2 circles (½-in/1-cm thick). Place 1 pie shell on bottom of a 9-in (23-cm) pie pan, then pour in berry mixture. Place second pie shell on top and pinch top and bottom together. Prick surface all over with a fork, then bake for 25 minutes until crust is golden brown. Cool completely, then refrigerate for 3 hours to allow berries to set.

Makes 6 servings.

Blackberry Mousse

Serve with whipped cream and crushed graham crackers.

2 envelopes unflavored gelatin (¼ oz/7 g each)
½ cup caster (superfine) sugar
Dash of salt
Water (for double boiler)
1½ cups blackberry juice
Large bowl of ice cubes
Yolks of 4 large eggs
¼ cup white sugar
Whites of 4 large eggs
¼ cup white sugar
1½ cups whipping cream
½ cup white sugar

In a bowl, combine gelatin, ½ cup sugar, and salt, mix well, and set aside. In the bottom pot of a double boiler on high heat, bring some water to a boil (ensure water does not touch top pot). In the top pot, slowly combine blackberry juice with gelatin mixture and bring to a boil. Continue boiling for 20 minutes, stirring continually until gelatin dissolves and mixture thickens. Remove from heat, and set pot in an ice bath, stirring mixture occasionally, for 15 minutes. In a bowl of an electric mixer on high, beat egg yolks for 3 minutes. Gradually add ¼ cup sugar and beat until very thick. In a separate bowl of an electric mixer on high, beat egg whites and ¼ cup sugar until soft peaks form. Gently fold egg white mixture into gelatin mixture until just combined, then set aside. In a bowl, beat cream with ½ cup sugar and fold gently into gelatin mixture. Pour into 4 individual dessert dishes. Refrigerate for 3 hours before serving.

Makes 4 servings.

Sopalali Mousse (Yel'iss)

Traditionally, this dessert was whipped by hand inside the feast house. Fireweed syrup was used to sweeten the sopalali froth, otherwise it is very bitter. Sopalali bushes are native to North America and usually nestle under Jack Pine trees. They measure about 4 feet (1¼ meters) high and have fragrant, velvety leaves. The red berries can be whipped, preserved, and dried. Fully ripe sopalali berries are squeezed or mashed.

2 tsp sopalali purée (see notes)
½ cup ice water
4 tsp white sugar
2 tsp Blackberry or Raspberry Syrup (page 177 or 176)

In a stainless steel mixing bowl, mix purée and water, then whip for 1 minute into a delicate pink consistency. Add sugar and whip for 1 additional minute. Divide mousse into 2 sugar-rimmed glasses. Pour syrup over top and serve immediately (see note).

Makes 2 servings.

- Sopalali is the common name of the soapberry plant in British Columbia. Sopalali is derived from "soopolallie," a word from the Chinook trading jargon—"soop" for soap and "olallie" for berry—used among Pacific Northwest peoples and settlers in the nineteenth and early twentieth centuries.

- Sopalali purée is available from gourmet food stores and distributors or from online sources.

- If you let the mousse stand for more than 3 minutes, it will separate and not whip together again, so serve it immediately.

Gitk'san Slush (Diy'ks)

During winter when Dolly was growing up, she and other children couldn't wait until it snowed so they could enjoy this dessert. This is a very old Gitk'san recipe, dating back to the pre-contact era. For the wild berries, try any combination of strawberries, raspberries, blackberries, and blueberries. If you'd like, sweeten this dessert with sugar.

4 cups fresh snow (or finely crushed ice)
2 tbsp oolichan oil (see note)
1 cup wild berries
2 tsp cold water

Place snow into a bowl. Add oil and water and whip into a froth. Fold in berries and serve immediately.

Makes 2 servings.

■ Wild berries mixed only with oolichan oil is called "glaya<u>x</u>."

■ See page 166 for information on making oolichan oil, or oolichan oil may be bought from specialty seafood markets or from online sources.

Gitk'san Fruit Salad

At feasts, this fruit salad is served by the gallons. Women either make their own at home, or bring their preserves and pour them all into one large communal container. Any leftovers are passed around to take home; some women even bring empty quart jars with this in mind. For the wild berries in this recipe, try raspberries, strawberries, blueberries, and/or blackberries.

2½ cups Pear & Apple Preserves (page 170)
½ cup orange sections
1 can applesauce (5 oz/150 ml)
2 cups wild berries
Whipped cream (for garnish)

In a bowl, combine all ingredients except garnish. Top each serving with whipped cream.

Makes 5 servings.

Wild Blueberry Cobbler (page 137)

Sopalali Mousse (page 142)

Smoked oolichan (page 65)

Smoked Salmon Strips (page 163)

Gitsegukla Wedding Cake

Dolly's grandmother, Elizabeth, used to make this simple raisin cake that uses bannock dough for the weddings held in Gitsegukla, a Gitk'san village just east of Terrace, in central British Columbia. Dolly made this cake for her own recent marriage to the mayor of Port Alberni, British Columbia.

½ cup raisins
½ cup sweetened dried cranberries
1½ cups boiling water
1¾ cups all-purpose flour
1½ tsp baking powder
¼ tsp baking soda
½ tsp salt
Pinch of nutmeg

Pinch of allspice
½ cup butter
¾ cup white sugar
1 large egg
2 tbsp all-purpose flour (for coating)
2½ cups Lemony Cream Cheese
    Frosting (below)
1 cup hazelnuts, chopped (for garnish)

Preheat oven to 350°F (180°C). Cover an 8x8x2-in (20x20x5-cm) baking pan with non-stick cooking spray, then line with parchment paper. In a saucepan on high heat, combine raisins, cranberries, and water and bring to a boil. Remove from heat and set aside to cool. In a large bowl, sift together 1¾ cups flour, baking powder, baking soda, salt, nutmeg, and allspice and mix, then set aside. In another bowl, cream together butter and sugar and set aside. In a third bowl, beat egg, then add to creamed mixture and mix, then set aside. Strain raisins and cranberries and place in a small bowl. Coat with 2 tbsp flour and set aside. Combine flour mixture and creamed mixture and mix well, then stir in floured raisins and cranberries. Place dough in prepared baking pan and bake for 35 minutes. Remove from oven and let cool for 5 minutes, then remove from pan. Once cake has completely cooled, frost with Cream Cheese Frosting and sprinkle with hazelnuts.

Makes 10 servings.

LEMONY CREAM CHEESE FROSTING

1 cup plain cream cheese
3 cups confectioner's (icing) sugar

½ tsp lemon extract
2 tbsp half-and-half cream

In the bowl of an electric mixer on high, combine all ingredients and cream together. Keep in a cool place until ready to use.

Makes 2½ cups.

Chocolate Pecan Cake with Caramel Pecan Sauce

This is a perfect and easy-to-make cake to satisfy your chocolate cravings. The pecans and chocolate add elegance and a delicious, decadent, and nutty taste with a truly divine combination of caramel sauce and fluffy chocolate frosting.

¾ cup margarine

¾ cup all-vegetable shortening

¼ cup unsweetened cocoa powder

½ cup boiling water

2 cups self-rising flour

1 cup caster (superfine) sugar
   (see note)

Yolks of 2 large eggs

1 cup Crème Fraîche (page 127)

1 tsp caramel extract

1 tsp allspice

1 tsp salt

1½ tsp instant coffee granules

Whites of 2 large eggs

½ tsp cream of tartar

1 cup Caramel Pecan Sauce (next page)

1¼ cups Chocolate Frosting (next page)

½ cup whole pecans (for garnish)

Preheat oven to 350°F (180°C). Cover 2 round cake pans (9x2-in/23x5-cm) with non-stick cooking spray and line with parchment paper. In the bottom pot of a double boiler on high heat, bring some water to a boil (ensure water does not touch the top pot). In top pot, combine margarine, shortening, and cocoa powder and melt, stirring continually until smooth. Remove from heat, add boiling water, and let stand for 15 minutes. In the bowl of an electric mixer on high, with a paddle attachment, combine flour, sugar, egg yolks, crème fraîche, caramel extract, allspice, salt, and coffee granules and blend together. In a stainless steel bowl, whip egg whites and cream of tartar until stiff peaks form. Fold into the flour mixture and then blend in chocolate mixture. Pour into prepared pans and spread evenly with a spatula. Bake uncovered for 35 minutes, then cover with tinfoil and bake for an additional 10 minutes. When done, loosen sides with a knife and turn cakes onto cooling racks. Remove from pans, peel off parchment paper, and let cakes cool completely. Once completely cooled, spread caramel sauce on top of one cake. Top with second cake, then frost top and sides using a palette knife and sprinkle pecans on top.

Makes 8 servings.

■ You can use berry sugar instead of caster.

■ To make cupcakes, preheat oven to 350°F (180°C). Divide cake batter evenly into 24 cupcake tins. Bake for 20 minutes.

CARAMEL PECAN SAUCE

¾ cup brown sugar
2 tsp golden corn syrup
½ cup Crème Fraîche (page 127)
¼ cup butter
1 oz (30 g) pecans, ground
1 tsp caramel extract
½ tsp allspice

In a heavy saucepan on high heat, combine sugar and syrup, bring to a boil and continue to boil for 5 minutes. Remove from heat and add crème fraîche and butter. Return to high heat and stir continually for 2 minutes. Remove from heat and stir in pecans, caramel extract, and allspice. Cool completely to room temperature before using.

Makes 1 cup.

CHOCOLATE FROSTING

½ cup cream cheese, softened
2 tbsp butter, softened
3 tbsp whipping cream
1 tbsp unsweetened cocoa powder
2 cups confectioner's (icing) sugar
½ tsp caramel extract

In the bowl of an electric mixer on high, combine cream cheese, butter, and whipping cream, and blend until creamed. In another bowl, combine cocoa powder, sugar, and caramel extract and mix. Add cocoa mixture to cream mixture and mix well. Keep in a cool place until ready to use.

Makes 1¼ cups.

War Cake

This recipe is from Dolly's late mother-in-law Peggy McRae of Port Alberni, British Columbia. It was a favorite during World War II, hence the name, when eggs were rationed and she would have to trade them for raisins.

1 cup raisins
2 cups boiling water
1½ tsp baking powder
1 tsp baking soda
1 tbsp lard
1½ cups all-purpose flour
1 cup white sugar
1 tsp allspice
¼ tsp salt
2½ cups Lemony Cream Cheese Frosting (page 145)
1 cup pecans, chopped (for garnish)

Preheat oven to 350°F (180°C). In a saucepan on high heat, combine raisins and water and bring to a boil, then reduce heat to low and simmer for 20 minutes. Stir in the baking powder, baking soda, and lard, then remove from heat and let cool. In a bowl, combine flour, sugar, allspice, and salt, then add raisin mixture. Pour into a lightly greased 8x8x2-in (20x20x5-cm) cake pan and bake for 25 minutes. Remove from oven and let cool completely. Once completely cooled, ice with frosting and sprinkle pecans on top.

Makes 10 servings.

Cranberry Hazelnut Drop Cookies

These cookies are great for luncheons or a light dessert.

1 large egg
5/8 cup all-purpose flour
¼ tsp baking soda
3/8 cup brown sugar
¼ cup butter, softened
½ tsp caramel extract
¼ tsp salt
Pinch of allspice
¼ cup hazelnuts, finely chopped
½ cup sweetened dried cranberries

Preheat oven to 375°F (190°C). Cover baking sheet with non-stick cooking spray. In a large bowl, beat egg until frothy. Add remaining ingredients and mix well. For each cookie, drop 1 tbsp of batter onto baking sheet. Bake for 15 minutes. Remove from oven and let cool.

Makes 12 cookies.

Nature's Desserts

SALMON BERRY SHOOTS

In early spring, the Tseshaht children on Vancouver Island pick tender young salmon berry shoots about 1 foot/30 cm high. (If the shoots are taller than 2 feet/60 cm, they are too tough and have a woody taste.) They peel back the thin, prickly outer layer and eat the translucent, tender green stems raw, dipping them in sugar. Salmon berries are salmon-red and resemble blackberries, and are sweet and juicy. Jam and jelly can be made from the salmon berries that ripen in the summertime.

PINE SAP

In early spring, the Gitk'san children in Kitwanga scrape pine sap off Jack Pine trees, which they called "pine noodles." The pine sap is collected before daybreak when it is milky and easy to extract because after the sun warms the bark, the "noodles" become too sticky. The outer bark of a young tree is cut off in small pieces and the juicy inner bark is scraped off with a bone scraper. Water-repellant spruce-root baskets are used to transport the pine sap. The children break off pieces of sap and chew it like gum. Pine sap is also great for mountain climbers, as it makes a good survival food.

STONE CROP (T'IP YEEST)

Stone crop is a delicious succulent plant with yellow flowers and is native to the Pacific Coast region. It is a type of rubber plant with small, bulbous, deep green leaves and succulent, fleshy stems and buds, and grows in abundance on the rocks near Kispiox, British Columbia. Dolly and her brothers and sisters would pick stone crop during the month of May, before it flowered; they would eat it by dipping it in sugar and oolichan oil.

Beverages

Sopalali Cranberry Punch

Sopalali are also known as soapberries or Canada buffaloberries. These bitter red berries grow on bushes generally found under Jack Pine trees. They are native to North America and are collected mostly by members of the Thompson River and Shuswap nations in British Columbia. Sopalali are often mixed with sweeter fruit like cranberries, raspberries, blackberries, or strawberries.

½ tsp sopalali purée (see note)
3¾ cups cranberry juice
Ice cubes
1½ cups ginger ale

In a container with a lid, combine sopalali purée and cranberry juice and shake well. Pour into 6 glasses with ice and top each with ginger ale.

Makes 6 cups.

■ Sopalali purée is available from gourmet markets and distributors or from online sources.

■ **Firewater Martini**: In a martini shaker with ice, combine 2½ oz vodka and 5 oz Sopalali Cranberry Punch (without the ginger ale) and shake well. Strain into 2 chilled martini glasses and top each with ginger ale. Makes 2 servings.

Saskatoon Berry Tea

Saskatoon berries are native to Western Canada, parts of Alaska, and the northwest United States; these sweet berries look like small blueberries. This blend of tea is delicate and flowery when Saskatoon berries are combined with rosehips, strawberries, black currants, blueberries, and hibiscus.

1 tbsp Saskatoon berry loose-leaf tea (see note)
4 cups boiling water
Honey (optional)

In a teapot, combine tea and boiling water. Let steep for 5 minutes. Stir to make sure flavor is uniform and serve. Sweeten with honey, if desired. (The ingredients are edible, so there is no need to strain, but remember: do not use milk or cream in this tea as it will curdle.)

Makes 4 servings.

■ We purchase Saskatoon Berry Loose Leaf Tea from Gramma Bep's Gourmet Foods in Swift Current, Saskatchewan. We met Mrs Bep at a farmer's market in Vancouver where we were both selling our goods. You may also find Saskatoon berry tea in specialty teashops or natural foods grocers.

SASKATOON BERRY BOUQUET ICED TEA

4 tsp Saskatoon berry loose-leaf tea
4 cups boiling water
3 tbsp honey
2 tsp lemon juice
Ice cubes

In a teapot, combine tea and boiling water. Let steep for 5 minutes. Strain into a tempered glass pitcher, then stir in honey and lemon juice and let cool. Serve over ice cubes in tall glasses.

Makes 4 servings.

Pine Needle Tea

This recipe makes a beautiful red tea with a mild pleasant taste. Use the needles from Jack Pines where available—preferably the bushy, younger-growth ones at the tip of the branches.

4 tsp pine needles, dried and loosely ground
4 cups boiling water
Honey (optional)

In a teapot, combine needles and boiling water, and let steep for 10 minutes. Strain and serve. Sweeten with honey, if desired.

Makes 4 servings.

■ For variation, add grated orange peel or nutmeg, cinnamon, and cloves.

Pacific West Coast Hemlock Tea

This tall evergreen is indigenous to North America and abundant in Pacific coastal forests. Pacific West Coast Hemlock, also known as Western Hemlock or Pacific Hemlock, is not the same as what most people know as hemlock, which is a poisonous plant from Europe. Pacific West Coast Hemlock is available year round, but the springtime needles make the best tea.

4 tsp Pacific West Coast Hemlock needles, dried and loosely ground
4 cups boiling water

In a teapot, combine needles and boiling water, and let steep for 20 minutes. Strain and serve.

Makes 4 servings.

■   For variation, mix this tea with dried licorice fern to taste.

Blackberry Leaf Tea

Blackberry leaves for tea are at their best in winter when they are old and turning red; they also have many health benefits.

2 tbsp blackberry leaves, dried and crumbled
4 cups boiling water
Honey (optional)

In a teapot, combine leaves (watch out for sharp spines) and boiling water, and let steep for 5 minutes. Strain and sweeten with honey, if desired.

Makes 4 servings.

■ For more color and a sharper taste, add a few fresh blackberries.

BLACKBERRY LEAF ICED TEA

¼ cup blackberry leaves, dried and crumbled
6 cups boiling water
¼ cup honey
Ice cubes

In a teapot, combine leaves (watch out for sharp spines) and boiling water, and let steep for 5 minutes. Strain into a tempered glass pitcher, discard leaves, then stir in honey and let cool. Serve over ice cubes in tall glasses.

Makes 6 servings.

BLACKBERRY-APPLE ICED TEA

6 cups Blackberry Leaf Iced Tea (see above)
2 cups apple juice
2 tsp pineapple juice
2 cups ginger ale
Ice cubes

In a glass pitcher, combine all ingredients. Serve over ice cubes in tall glasses.

Makes 10 servings.

Fireweed Tea

Fireweed is a wild herb that can be found throughout North America. The fireweed plant grows 4 to 6 feet (1¼ to 1¾ meters) tall and bears pink flowers. The plant got its name because it is often the first plant to grow back after a forest fire. In Alaska, candies, syrups, and jellies are made from fireweed. Its leaves may be picked at anytime; however, the best tea comes from leaves picked right before the fireweed plant flowers in early summer. Fireweed leaves can be used either fresh or dried, but this tea is best when using dried.

3 tbsp fireweed leaves, dried and crushed (see note)
4 cups boiling water
Cinnamon (optional)
Nutmeg (optional)

In a teapot, combine leaves and boiling water and let steep for 10 minutes. Flavor with cinnamon or nutmeg, if desired.

Makes 4 servings.

- This tea may be blended with other wild herbs such as mint, rosehip, sheep sorrel, or strawberry.

- Fireweed can be purchased from specialty herb or tea stores or from online sources.

Homemade Root Beer

Kids have lots of fun making this root beer. Dolly remembers that when her mother made it, she let it carbonate by lowering it into a well.

1½ cups corn sugar (dextrose)
1½ cups brown sugar
¼ tsp powdered baker's yeast
1 tbsp root beer extract
Tepid water (to fill bottles)

Sterilize a 2-liter plastic soda bottle and a screw cap to avoid bacterial growth. Funnel corn sugar, brown sugar, and yeast into the bottle and shake to mix. Funnel extract and enough tepid water to fill bottle half-full and shake until all ingredients are dissolved. Add more tepid water to fill bottle, leaving ½-in (1¼-cm) headspace. Screw cap on and let cool ensuring the bottle is upright. Store in a warm place for 5 days to allow root beer to carbonate, then refrigerate and drink within 2 weeks.

Makes 2 liters.

Smoked Foods & Preserves

Traditional Ways of Smoking and Preserving Fish and Wild Game

It is tradition among many nations of indigenous people in North America to smoke, dry in the open air, and preserve foods to last all year-round, yet each nation has its own unique methods of preparing and preserving. In our Gitk'san culture, the entire family is involved in hunting and gathering food to smoke and preserve. Generally, the men catch the salmon, starting with the spring salmon run, then sockeye and coho, and ending in late August with the final run of the chum salmon (also known as dog salmon). Oolichan, small silvery fish that migrate in the millions in many mainland rivers in British Columbia, are caught in early spring with nets. Herring, found in inland waters of the Pacific Ocean, are abundant in March. Once the fish are harvested, it is usually up to the women to prepare them for smoking.

Fish and wild game are traditionally smoked in a smokehouse ("wilp sa hon") made of cedar. The preparers use cedar skewers, poles, or racks to hang the whole fish or meat or fish fillets or strips vertically, inside the smokehouse above a slow-burning alder wood fire. Alder wood is the best wood for smoking because its smoke does not discolor the food and it emits a steady, low heat, but cottonwood and poplar wood are also used. As the meat smokes, it has to be turned daily to dehydrate and cure evenly, while ensuring the meat does not overheat (if it does overheat, it has to be cooked and eaten immediately, otherwise it will spoil). The men often help in this process by hanging the fish or meat in the smokehouse or in the open air (with a fire built close by) and gathering the wood for the fire.

There are two gradients to smoking fish and meats: fully smoked (or simply "smoked") or half-smoked. Food is considered half-smoked when the moisture content is reduced by fifty percent. Half-smoked foods are more moist and softer than the drier, fully smoked foods and because of this, half-smoked foods should be eaten right away or stored in a freezer. Fully smoked foods have a stronger, smokier taste and are completely dehydrated, with the consistency of jerky. Overall, the smoking process requires patience and attention. The amount of smoking time depends greatly on the size of fish and the degree of smokiness desired: for example, a half-smoked whole salmon

only takes two days, but does not keep as long as the fully smoked salmon strips, which require five days. Fully smoked whole salmon ("gwelgwa hun") takes six days; herring generally requires two days. Additionally, each individual type of salmon has a special way of being smoked and preserved, depending on the type of its flesh. Spring salmon is usually half-smoked, for example, while sockeye, coho, or chum are half- or fully smoked.

Traditionally in our culture, smoking is the most popular method of fish and wild game preservation; however, drying it in the open air as it smokes is another way to make it last throughout the winter. For example, oolichan and salmon are wind-dried and smoked—or "dry smoked"—outside when the weather is dry and sunny (food should not get wet during the drying process). The food is hung up (high enough to keep away from animals) using cedar skewers, bark ropes, or poles, with a fire built close by to keep insects away and impart a slightly smoky flavor. It is important to fully dehydrate it until there is no moisture left in order to prevent mildew, souring, or decay. The process of dry-smoking depends on the size and cut of fish or game; for example, fully dry-smoked oolichan require five days, and fully dry-smoked salmon strips ("ghy'hooks") require five days. Foods can also be smoked in the smokehouse first and then dry-smoked in the open air. For example, venison strips require one day of smoking in the smokehouse, then four days of dry-smoking outdoors.

Traditionally, smoked or dry-smoked foods are stored in a wooden box or wrapped in birch bark then buried in a cool, dry-earth cellar that is lined and covered with birch bark. Rocks are piled on top of the wrapped food to prevent animals and insects from getting to it. Today, fully smoked foods can be stored in a sealed container in the refrigerator or in a cool, dry place for up to one year; half-smoked foods, which are not fully dehydrated, may keep in the freezer for up to one year.

Note: The following smoking "recipes" are admittedly ambitious, and are largely included here as points of information.

Smoked (Kippered) Herring

Prepare herring for smoking by running your thumbnail through the thin stomach skins to scrape out and discard the innards. Wash herring thoroughly in cold water. Kipper them by rubbing salt on them. Make a slit at the base of the tails. Fold tails over and push through slits.

On cedar skewers, skewer herring through the slits and place skewers horizontally between 2 poles situated above a fire in a smokehouse. Hang fish vertically, ensuring they are high enough from flames so they do not overheat. Turn fish occasionally to ensure herring smoke and dry evenly. Herring is fully smoked in 2 days.

Reconstitute smoked herring by soaking in cold water overnight. Boil for 3 minutes, drain and pat dry. Serve with potatoes, buttered bread, and a wedge of lemon.

Smoked Salmon Strips (Ghy'hooks)

Prepare fresh, whole salmon to be fully smoked by wiping with a clean, damp cloth. Cut off head and fins, leaving tail on. Cut open and gut belly and remove spine and keep for making Salmon Stock (page 106). Fillet flesh into strips, about ¼-in (1-cm) thick. In a smokehouse, drape salmon strips vertically over a pole above a slow-burning alder wood fire. Smoke for 5 days to fully smoke, turning occasionally to smoke evenly. Fully smoked salmon strips last up to 1 year without refrigeration; store in a wooden box or sealed container in a cool, dry place.

Reconstitute smoked salmon strips by soaking them overnight in water or covering them with boiling water. As part of a meal, smoked salmon strips can be served with potatoes, rice, green onions, and vegetables. Or, for roasted smoked salmon strips, pre-heat oven to 375°F (190°C). On a baking sheet, place reconstituted, smoked salmon strips and roast for 5 minutes. Break off into pieces and eat as is, or lightly salt and dip in melted butter or oolichan oil (see page 166).

- Elders often use fern leaves to clean the fish instead of water because they believe that the water rinses away too much flavor.

Smoked Whole Salmon (Gwelgwa Hun)

Prepare whole salmon to be fully smoked by wiping with a clean, damp cloth. Cut off head and fins, leaving tail on. Cut open to gut belly and remove spine and keep for making Salmon Stock (page 106). In a smokehouse, hang salmon vertically above a slow-burning alder wood fire. Smoke for 2 days, turning occasionally to smoke evenly. Trim away thicker parts of salmon that may not be smoking well, skewer them and rest of the fish with ½-in (1¼-cm) thick cedar skewers. Hang on cedar racks to smoke for an additional 4 days, until salmon has hardened. Fully smoked salmon lasts up to 1 year without refrigeration; store in a wooden box or sealed container in a cool, dry place.

To serve, roast smoked salmon (in its dried form, do not reconstitute) skin-side down over an open fire until the skin begins to get crispy and the natural oils begin to surface. Turn salmon over and roast flesh-side down for an additional minute. Season with salt, if desired, and serve with Just Like Grandma's Bannock (page 130), cold boiled potatoes, and chopped onions.

Half-Smoked Whole Salmon (Jh'el)

Prepare whole salmon for half-smoking by wiping with a clean, damp cloth. Cut off head and fins, leaving tail on. Cut open to gut belly and remove spine and keep for making Salmon Stock (page 106). In a smokehouse, hang salmon vertically above a slow-burning alder wood fire. Smoke overnight, turning occasionally to smoke evenly. Trim away thicker parts of salmon that may not be smoking well, skewer them and the rest of the fish with ½-in (1¼-cm) thick cedar skewers. Hang on cedar racks to smoke for an additional day; salmon should be moist and soft. Half-smoked salmon lasts up to 1 year in a sealed container in the freezer. Half-smoked whole salmon is used in the Wild Smoked Salmon Cream Cheese recipe on page 112.

To serve, poach or bake the half-smoked whole salmon and serve with rice or potatoes. Drizzle oolichan oil (see note) over the hot salmon.

■ See page 166 for information on making oolichan oil, or it may be purchased from specialty seafood markets or from online sources. You may substitute with seal oil.

Oolichan Oil

Oolichan oil is used as a dip for potatoes, salmon berry shoots, smoked salmon, seaweed, and salmon roe. It is also added to salmon or seal soup. When processed properly, oolichan oil may be stored in a sealed container in a cool, dry place for up to 1 year.

Extract the oil by placing freshly caught oolichan in a cedar box that is built over the riverbank and has cedar boughs lining the bottom of the box. Cover box and leave oolichan to "ripen" for 7–10 days, depending on the weather (the warmer the weather, the quicker the flesh will "ripen," allowing the oils to surface). Transfer oolichan to a large pot of boiling water. Allow fish to boil, stirring every few minutes to release oil until oolichan are cooked, then add cold water to stop cooking process and allow oil to rise to the surface. Let sit for several hours to allow sediment to sink and oil to rise. Strain oil through several layers of cheesecloth, allowing pure oil to drain into sterilized gallon jugs. Seal jugs and store in a cool, dry place. Alternately, drain oil into sealable containers and store in the refrigerator or freezer.

- The Gitk'san often harvested oolichan (also spelled "oolican" or "eulachon" and sometimes called "candle fish") from the Nass River. Rich in oils, oolichan have a high food value and the Gitk'san consider them "the little friend to all the world."

Pemmican Balls

Pemmican consists of smoked and dried meat (usually venison) that has been pounded into a powder and mixed with hot fat and dried fruits or berries, then pressed into either a loaf or small cakes or balls. Traditionally, bags of pemmican were stored inside rawhide and placed in the stomachs of wild game (with its fur left on) that are sewn up tightly then buried in the ground at strategic points on the hunting trail. This method kept the pemmican fresh during the winter; in fact, it could be edible for years. Pemmican can be made from other meats such as buffalo, moose, or beef.

2½ lbs (3 kg) venison (hind-quarters or shoulders are best)
2 cups rendered fat from venison, liquefied
5 cups wild berries, dried and ground to powder (may substitute with conventional raspberries, blackberries, blueberries, cranberries, or strawberries) (see note)

Cut venison into strips and skewer onto cedar skewers. In a smokehouse, place skewers above a slow-burning alder wood fire overnight, turning occasionally to smoke meat evenly. When meat feels hard to the touch, remove it from smokehouse and place the skewers on poles so meat can hang outdoors in sunny weather with a fire nearby to dry-smoke for an additional 4 days. In a food processor, grind meat until it has the consistency of powder. In a bowl, combine meat, fat, and berries and mix well. Form pemmican into balls (1-in/2½-cm in diameter) and store in sealed containers in the freezer.

Makes 40 balls.

■ To naturally dry fresh berries, on a hot day place berries on an elevated board outdoors and allow the sun to dry them.

Traditional Way of Making Preserves

In Gitk'san culture, during spring and summer months, the women and children would pick berries that grew locally, or take longer journeys into the mountains to collect them. (Mountains on the six Gitk'san territories are owned by "houses" such as the Gitk'san Wolf, Frog, Eagle, and Fireweed. The man who owns the mountain gives permission to his wife, who belongs to another "house," for family members to pick berries, hunt, or fish in that region.) Once the wild berries are harvested, the first step in preparing them for jam, jelly, or sauces that will keep all year-round is to crush them, then strain the berry juice (which also makes a great cool drink by adding 1 cup water and ½ cup sugar to the juice of 2-qt/2-l crushed berries). The crushed berries are then placed in a strong wooden box. Stones are heated over a fire until red hot, then lifted using a carved cedar plank that is split down the middle, and dropped in the wooden box with the crushed berries. The hot stones cook the berries, which are turned often for 20 minutes. The women then pour the cooked berries over a "dryer": skunk cabbage leaves that are spread over cedar planks, with a small fire glowing beneath. The dried berries are then pressed down and cut into "cakes" about ½-in (1¼-cm) thick and cut into bite-sized pieces, or rolled into a large cylinder shape and stored in a wooden box. The cakes would often be traded for seafood from the coastal aboriginal people, or make a handy snack to take along on hunting or trapping trips.

Today, we continue the rich tradition of preserving foods, but with modern appliances and methods to make jams, jellies, fruit spreads, relishes, chutneys, sauces, vinegars, and condiments.

To can preserves: Use only the best quality fruits and vegetables to preserve them at their peak of ripeness. Mason jars made of tempered glass to withstand the hot then cold processes are the best type to use for canning. Before starting, discard any jars with cracks or chips, as these defects can prevent sealing. Do not re-use jar lids. (If not using Mason jars, lids, and screwbands, follow manufacturer's instructions for canning.) To sterilize jars, place them on a rack and immerse them into boiling water for 5 minutes. Remove and fill jars with hot-packed or fresh food, leaving ½-in (1¼-cm) headspace. Remove air bubbles by sliding a nonmetallic utensil between food and glass and pressing gently on food to release trapped air. Wipe jar rim clean and place lid on with sealing compound next to glass. Screw the metal screwband tightly by hand; do not over-tighten, as the contents will expand and the lid needs enough give to allow gasses or air to "vent" from jars during processing. To seal jars, use a water-bath canner with a flat bottom, rack, and lid on an electric range. Preheat enough water in canner that will cover jars by 1 in (2½ cm) to boiling point (212°F/100°C), then immerse jars. Cover and continue boiling water, maintaining this temperature for the entire processing time to prevent contamination with bacteria and other microorganisms. For pint-sized jars, boil for 15 minutes, and for quart-sized, boil for 20 minutes—making sure to start counting processing time once water returns to a rolling boil after immersing jars. With a jar-lifter, remove jars from water and place them set apart and upside-down on a folded tea towel. Leave undisturbed overnight to allow them to cool, drain, and form a strong vacuum seal. There is no need to tighten the metal screwband after taking jars from canner. Jars have successfully been vacuum-sealed when the lids are curved downward and do not move when pressed. Reprocess or refrigerate any unsealed jars. For all sealed jars, remove screwbands and wipe dry both bands and jars. Replace bands loosely on jars. Label and store jars in a dry, cool place for up to 1 year.

Pear & Apple Preserves

Growing up, Annie remembers her family's pantry always being full of preserves. The warm weather of Port Alberni helps to grow deliciously sweet pears. These canned sweet pears and apples also make a great crisp or cobbler or used in the Gitk'san Fruit Salad (page 144).

2½ cups boiling water
3 cups white sugar
¾ cup Bartlett pears, peeled, cored, and cut into bite-sized pieces
¾ cup Granny Smith apples, peeled, cored, and cut into bite-sized pieces
1 tbsp pineapple juice
Pinch of nutmeg

In a saucepan on high heat, combine water and sugar and bring to a boil. Continue to boil for 10 minutes, stirring continually until it thickens to a syrup. Place pears and apples into sterilized Mason jars and cover with hot syrup, juice, and nutmeg. Preserve as directed on page 169 (you may want to increase the recipe quantity before preserving).

Makes 2½ cups.

Savory Wild Blueberry Jam

Abundant around Port Alberni on Vancouver Island, wild blueberries are smaller in size than conventional, farmed blueberries. Serve this savory jam with wild game dishes such as Alder-Grilled Marinated Elk (page 16) or Alder-Grilled Marinated Venison Chops (page 17).

½ tsp sunflower oil
½ cup Blackberry Syrup (page 177)
¼ tsp salt
¼ tsp black pepper
⅛ cup onions, diced
½ tsp dried rosemary
1 cup wild blueberries (may substitute with conventional blueberries)

In a saucepan on medium, heat oil. Add syrup, salt, pepper, onions, and rosemary and sauté for 2 minutes. Add berries and allow mixture to come to a boil for an additional 2 minutes. Reduce heat to low and simmer, stirring continually for 20 minutes. Let cool, then store in a sealed container in the refrigerator, or preserve as directed on page 169 (you may want to increase the recipe quantity before preserving).

Makes ¾ cup.

Festive Cranberry-Cherry Jam

Serve with the Stuffed Duck Roll (page 32), Oven-Roasted Duck (page 34), or Alder-Grilled Marinated Duck Breast (page 35). This jam can also be served with turkey or chicken dishes in place of traditional cranberry sauce.

¾ cup cranberries
¾ cup sweetened dried pitted cherries
2 tbsp cranberry juice
2 tbsp pineapple juice
½ cup Raspberry Syrup (page 176)
½ cup white sugar
1 tbsp orange zest
¼ cup onions, finely diced
1 clove garlic, minced
1 tsp allspice
1 tbsp butter

In a heavy saucepan on medium heat, combine all ingredients and simmer for 20 minutes, stirring continually. Let cool, then store in a sealed container in the refrigerator, or preserve as directed on page 169 (you may want to increase the recipe quantity before preserving).

Makes 2½ cups.

Rhubarb-Strawberry Jam

This jam is a sweet and tangy combination of rhubarb and strawberries. Both of these fruits grow at the same time in spring and early summer. Wild strawberries grew around the edges of our garden. Keep the leaves, as they make great hot or iced tea.

6 cups water
6 cups rhubarb, unpeeled, chopped
6 cups strawberries, hulled and sliced
1 cup apple cider vinegar
6 cups caster (superfine) sugar

In a large pot on high heat, bring water to boil. Reduce heat to low, add rhubarb and cover with lid. Simmer for 30 minutes, then drain. Add strawberries, vinegar, and sugar to rhubarb and increase heat to high to bring to a boil. Continue to boil for about 25 minutes, stirring continually until jam thickens. Remove from heat and pass through a food mill. Let cool, then store in a sealed container in the refrigerator, or preserve as directed on page 169 (you may want to increase the recipe quantity before preserving).

Makes 7 cups.

Crabapple & Raspberry Jam

Fresh ginger and cloves add delightful flavor and aroma to the rather neutral-tasting crabapples.

5 cups water
5 cups crabapples, peeled, cored, and chopped
3 whole cloves
1-in (2½-cm) fresh ginger, peeled and chopped
3 cups raspberries
¾ cup pineapple juice
6 cups caster (superfine) sugar

In a large pot on high heat, combine water, crabapples, cloves, and ginger and bring to a boil, continuing to boil for 10 minutes. Strain through a fine sieve into a bowl to remove and discard cloves and ginger. Return strained juice and crabapples to pot, add raspberries, juice, and sugar. Bring to a boil, stirring continually for 25 minutes until jam thickens. Let cool, then store in a sealed container in the refrigerator, or preserve as directed on page 169 (you may want to increase the recipe quantity before preserving).

Makes 6 cups.

Huckleberry Jam

Dolly used to pack smoked fish, roasted cedar-flavored tea, and warm blankets to take with her and her brothers and sisters to go huckleberry picking on a mountain called Sta'ghiy'it near their village, Kitwanga. Huckleberries look like small blueberries.

8 cups huckleberries
2 tbsp pineapple juice
5 cups white sugar

In a saucepan on high heat, combine huckleberries, juice, and sugar and bring to a boil. Reduce heat to medium and continue to boil, stirring continually for 20 minutes until jam thickens. Let cool, then store in a sealed container in the refrigerator, or preserve as directed on page 169 (you may want to increase the recipe quantity before preserving).

Makes 5 cups.

Raspberry Syrup

Use this syrup with the Sweet & Tangy Purple Cabbage (page 74), Sweet Raspberry Onions (page 75), Raspberry Cranberry Chutney (page 117), Tangy Rhubarb Sauce (page 113), and Festive Cranberry-Cherry Jam (page 172).

2 cups raspberries
1¼ cups white sugar
1 tsp pineapple juice

In a saucepan on high heat, combine all ingredients and bring to a boil. Reduce heat to medium and continue to cook at a low boil, stirring continually for 10 minutes until syrup thickens. (For an even thicker syrup for pancakes or waffles, simmer for an additional 5 minutes.) Remove from heat and let cool and store in a sealed container in the refrigerator.

Makes 1¾ cups.

Blackberry Syrup

Use this syrup with the Alder-Grilled Marinated Duck Breast (page 35), Pheasant in a Blanket (page 38), Blackberry Poppy Seed Dressing (page 79), Savory Wild Blueberry Jam (page 171), Blackberry-Glazed Beets (page 73), or Sopalali Mousse (page 142).

2 cups blackberries
1¼ cups white sugar
1 tsp pineapple juice

In a saucepan on high heat, combine all ingredients and bring to a boil. Reduce heat to medium and continue to cook at a low boil, stirring continually for 10 minutes until syrup thickens. (For an even thicker syrup for pancakes or waffles, simmer for an additional 5 minutes.) Remove from heat and let cool and store in a sealed container in the refrigerator.

Makes 1¾ cups.

Apple-Pear Butter

Serve this lightly spicy and sweet-tasting creamy butter with warm Just Like Grandma's Bannock (page 130) or Baked Bannock (page 131).

8 cups apple cider
6 cups Bartlett pears, peeled, cored, and chopped
2 cups white sugar
1 tsp allspice

In a saucepan on high heat, bring apple cider to a boil. Continue to boil for 1 hour, stirring occasionally. Reduce heat to medium, add pears, and cook for an additional 10 minutes. Add sugar and allspice and continue to cook, stirring continually for 25 minutes until butter thickens. Remove from heat and pass through a food mill. Preserve as directed on page 169 and store in a cool, dry place.

Makes 5 cups.

Index